A Beginner's Gu
in an RV

A BEGINNER'S GUIDE TO LIVING IN AN RV

Everything I Wish I Knew Before Full-Time RVing Across America

Alyssa Padgett

Padgett Creative LLC

ISBN: 9781973321514

To Mimi—
Thank you for always supporting this crazy
idea to live in a home on wheels. Love you
always.

CONTENTS

PRAISE FOR LIVING IN AN RV

Such a blessing Heath & Alyssa are for the newest generation of full-time RVers hitting the road and working remotely! We've been on the road ourselves for over a decade, and it's rare to encounter their tenacity for providing helpful, well thought out and informative content.
—*Chris and Cherie*, Technomadia

Alyssa Padgett's guide is packed with useful information for those looking to transition into the RV lifestyle. Not only does she take you on an educational journey by sharing knowledge from her experiences in an easy to read format, she will have you cracking up along the way!
—*Travis and Melanie*, Xscapers RV Club

If you're looking to start RV life, there is no one better to teach you how than Alyssa Padgett. Alyssa is well-known in the RVing community for her RV expertise and she's one of the nicest people I've met. This guide will help you with everything you need to know- from deciding what RV to buy to establishing a domicile, and even making sure that you're connected to internet while on the road. I highly recommend reading this!
—*Michelle Schroeder-Gardner*, Making Sense of Cents

Living in an RV is a good primer to a life on the road. Alyssa's compilation of her years full-time RVing makes a great read for anyone looking at the RV life.

—*Kerensa Durr*, RV to Freedom

If you are looking to have all of your questions answered about how to get on the road and live in your RV full time this is the guide for you! Alyssa does an amazing job getting into the details around all of the things you want to think about before diving into full-time RV living.

I only wish there was a guide like this when we started traveling full time! It definitely would have helped us and stopped us from making some bad decisions when we first got on the road. If you are in the planning stages, getting ready to launch or already on the road this guide will be useful in making the transition to full-time RV life!

—*Bryanna Royal*, Crazy Family Adventure

PROLOGUE

We pulled into our RV park with "Just Married" faintly legible on the back window of my car and parked next to a 20-year-old motorhome. This would be the first home of our marriage, the home that would take us to all fifty states. Well, 49 of them at the very least.

Heath didn't carry me across the threshold, since that would require carrying me up a questionable metal step that we would end up welding a few months down the road.

Four days into our marriage, we started the engine and drove away from Austin, Texas fully unprepared for the adventure ahead.

Now I've been a full-timer for nearly four years.

Sometimes, I say things like, I'm a full-timer, fully expecting that people know what that word means. (Actually, if there's anything I say in this book that you haven't heard of, check the glossary in the back of the book for definitions of common RVing terms.)

More often than not—and this is especially true when I talk to people in their twenties—no one knows what full-time RVing is.

And I can say with certainty that the general public definitely has no idea that there are people out there like us who full-time RV before retirement and grandkids and social security.

So what is full-time RVing? (And why is it the coolest thing you should be doing with your life right now?)

Full-time RVing or being a "full-timer" simply means I sleep all of my nights in my RV. It's my house, my only home, and that's all I've got.

"So how do you get your mail?"

This is literally the first question most people ask when I explain full-timing. Which, by the way, SUPER boring question. I live on wheels and you want to know about mail. Smh. But don't worry, I'll dig into mail in Part 2 of this book.

Back to full-time RVing and why it's awesome.

When you're a full-timer, you can:

- Not be tied down to mortgages, bills, and the monotony of staying in one place
- Live anywhere you want. (In our experience, this has included beachfront of the Pacific Ocean, riverfront, lakefront, mountainside, on a volcano, on farms, at wineries, in national forests, heck, we even took our rig to New York City!)
- Work from anywhere
- Meet new people
- Spend more time in nature
- Save a ton of money
- Basically do anything you want all the time

All this could be summed up very succinctly: Full-timing is the BEST.

Who full-time RVs? (And can we make RV a verb?)

In the past three years, I've met adults as young as 21 and as old as their 80s traveling full-time across the country. I've seen families with infants, teenagers, and more kids than I could ever imagine living with all piled into a trailer together.

Being a full-timer has nothing to do with age or means or where you're from. (In fact, RVing is even more popular abroad than it is here in the States.)

Full-timers are people who want to travel and see the world. They want total freedom from the financial ties like mortgages, physical ties like foundations, and social ties that expect you to keep up with the Joneses.

Why should you full-time RV?

In the past few decades, the world has changed in a million different ways. But the most overwhelming way is this: we have choices like no society has ever had before.

Your grocery store doesn't offer great avocados? There are probably five others equidistant from your house. You don't like Shell gas stations? You have a hundred other options. Nothing good on TV? Don't worry, there are only millions of tv shows and movies you can watch on cable or satellite or the Internet. You don't want to work from an office? You can work from home or a co-working space or Starbucks or a bar with wifi or in an RV on the coast (yeah, I've done all of these).

We have more options every day than we know what to do with. Living in an RV and traveling full time is just one of them.

And yet, everyone is living in a home with four walls and indoor plumbing. Across the board, most people I know live in what we RVers call a "sticks-and-bricks" or "brick-and-mortar" home. Which is great if you're worried about tornadoes or if you want a stable, predictable future, but it's not great if you want to get out and see the world and learn and grow and be a better person (all of these are side effects of full-time travel).

So you could be like everyone else and sit around complaining about property taxes and traffic and how you don't understand why everyone cares about the Kardashians because you don't care about the Kardashians, but no matter what you all still end up talking about the Kardashians.

Or, you can try full timing.

There weren't many resources for full-timers when we started our RV adventures. We threw caution to the wind and learned as we go. Which in retrospect seems a little wild and reckless, but it's better than sitting around dreaming about someday.

Who this guide is for

This guide is for anyone who wants to travel North America in an RV full-time. I will walk you through choosing your RV, understanding how it works, transitioning your life on the road (mail, insurance, and internet oh my!) and what it's really like living on the road.

What this guide isn't

This guide isn't a collection of stories about RVing. It isn't about traveling to all fifty states or picking the perfect places to visit on your next road trip.

This guide is designed to help you make the transition and answer all your biggest questions about life on the road. I'll share our experiences from the past three and a half years and our answers to the questions about RVing that we hear every day.

Let's dig in.

PART I

FINDING THE RIGHT RIG

1

EXPLORING YOUR RV OPTIONS

When we first started RV shopping, my husband had me convinced that a truck camper was right for us. He said it was the perfect size and our most affordable option. And I believed him because I had *no* idea what a truck camper was.

He was so wrong!

Not only was a truck camper way too small for us and not ideal for a full-time home, buying a truck and camper was going to be more expensive than our motorhome!

This is why it's important to do your research! So your husband can't trick you into bad ideas.

Your first RV is a daunting purchase and finding the right RV for you is so important. There a ton of options to choose from, but before you even go shopping, let's go over the different features of each.

To keep things simple, let's say there are three distinct types of RVs.

1. Motorhomes
2. Trailers
3. Campers

Now within these three types, there are quite a few different options. There are Class A's (or B's or C's). There are travel trailers and fifth wheels. Then there are always pop-up campers and truck campers. Or if you're really fancy, there are bus conversions and motorcoaches.

It starts getting confusing, doesn't it?

There's no single right answer to what RV is the best option. Different RVs are better for different people.

Let's break down these three categories.

Motorhomes

Motorhomes are exactly what they sound like: homes with motors. This is the key distinction (and just so you know for later, if you want to tow a car, this is the type of rig for you). Please don't confuse motorhomes with mobile homes. They are completely different. Mobile homes are what you see riding on the back of "oversized loads" going down the highway.

Trailers

Trailers are motorless RVs that must be towed by a truck or some other heavy-duty vehicle.

Campers

Campers[1] are everything that doesn't quite fall into these two options and are more designed for "weekenders" (i.e. people who don't use an RV as their primary residence, but use it purely for pleasure). Campers are typically smaller than trailers and more lightweight. You'll need to own a truck or just a large SUV for these.

Doesn't-Really-Fit-Anywhere-Else Secret Option #4: Toy Haulers

If you're into ATVs or motorcycles or extra space to convert into an office, consider a toy hauler. These are available as Class A motorhomes, travel trailers, Super C's, and most commonly in fifth wheels.

Class A Motorhomes

Average Length: 27 to 45 feet
Average Height: 11 feet to 13 foot 6 inches
Average Cost (new): $70K-$1M+

1. Campers is my catch-all term for RVs that don't easily lend themselves to full-time travel. Many campers are technically trailers, but since they are not designed for full-time use, campers is a more appropriate term.

Pros

- Ample living space
- Kitchen amenities: stove, oven, microwave, refrigerator
- Bathroom amenities: toilet, separated shower
- Sleeps 4+
- Inclusive
- Gas or diesel options available

Cons

- Expensive initial cost
- Motor maintenance
- Insurance costs (versus trailers)
- Length limits ability to travel certain place
- Need to tow a car for easier local travel

Class A's are your classic motorhome. Heath and I have owned and loved our Class A Winnebago Brave for the past 18 months When it comes to motorhomes, Class A's are your largest option. Generally speaking, they will have the highest-powered motors and offer the most space.

Class A's typically range between 27-45 feet long. Most A's will have at least one slide-out. The bigger the rig, the more specialty features you can expect. Our 33-foot rig with two slides (also referred to commonly as slide-outs or pop-outs) has a king-sized bed, a huge couch (that folds into a bed), dinette that seats four (and converts into a bed), a twin-size loft bed, and a removable coffee table.

Our rig sleeps five total, which is average for a Class A.

Layouts for Class A's will differ based on manufacturer and model. But 99% of Class A's will include a kitchen (refrigerator, sink, stove, oven, microwave), a bathroom (toilet, sink, shower), a dining table or dining table/couch combo, and a bedroom.

Depending on the year, some models might not have showers, and ovens are typically considered a "specialty" feature. But overall, it has everything your home would have, including two A/C units. Because it includes two A/Cs (one for the living area, one for the bedroom), Class A's run on 50 AMP power.

Most often, Class A's are gas, but there are diesel options. Overall, they are the most expensive type of RV and offer a great deal of space.

Class C Motorhomes

Average Length: 23 to 35 feet
Average Height: 10 to 11 feet
Average Cost (new): $50K-$120K

Pros

- Living space

- Kitchen amenities: stove, oven (in larger models), microwave, refrigerator
- Bathroom amenities: toilet, shower
- Sleeps 3+
- Inclusive

Cons

- Expensive initial cost
- Motor maintenance
- Insurance costs (versus trailers)
- Need/want to tow a car for easier local travel (unless you're comfortable driving the RV around)
- Less living space than Class A (even if rigs are the same length) because of the separated driving area

Class C motorhomes have a very distinct silhouette. While Class A's have giant windshields, Class C's have a loft above the cab. This loft is typically a bed or a storage option.

Class C's are generally shorter (in height and length) and smaller than Class A's. C's will have a kitchen and bathroom, but depending on the length, might not have a full bedroom. Your bed might be above the cab of the rig.

In general, you can expect less or smaller features in a C compared to an A. For example, no oven, a significantly smaller shower, and a kitchen table for two instead of four.

C's will run on 30 AMP power. Among other things, this means your C will have only one A/C unit. This also means you'll have better electric options when traveling. We often are forced to use 30 AMPs on our Class

A because of lack of availability of 50 AMP sites at RV parks.

The biggest difference between the A & C are the driving areas. You will always step down into a C driving area, and you will have driver and passenger doors in addition to the main door. Because you step down into this area, the cab isn't "livable" space, while it typically can be in an A. This means that even though many Class A's and C's are the same length, A's have more living space.

Engines between these two classes are very similar and sometimes even the exact same. If you trust my RV salesman, supposedly Class A engines get better gas mileage, even if they are identical engines. (What am I saying? He probably made that up.) C's are great for fast or moderate-paced travel, regardless of gas mileage. Depending on the length of your C, you'll likely want to tow a car.

Class B Motorhomes

Average Length: 15 to 25 feet
Average Height: 9 to 10 feet
Average Cost (new): $40K-$125K

Pros

- Small and easy to maneuver
- Great for fast-paced travel
- Sleeps 2(+)

Cons

- Small living area for more than two people
- Fewer amenities
- Motor maintenance
- Insurance costs
- Smallest amount of storage space in a motorhome
- They can often be as expensive as Class C's (but less space)

Class B's are smaller than A's and smaller than C's.

"That's weird. Why aren't the motorhomes named based on size?" I DON'T KNOW. It would only make sense for B's to be the medium sized rig. But this is how it is.

Class B's are your smallest motorhome option. But don't discount these bad boys based on their size. Many B's are up to 25 ft long.

B's can be luxury vehicles. Many are built on Mercedes chassis, so you'll have a diesel engine known for lasting. (Check out Leisure Travel Vans or Winnebago for examples of these.) This means they can be pricey since you're paying for a diesel engine, but in addition to the strong engines, some of the most beautiful RV interiors I've seen are inside B's.

To be clear, B's are NOT vans. They are slightly larger, but still able to fit in a parking space. I don't cover vans or van conversions in this book because vans and RVs are two different beasts and lifestyles. Vans will be smaller and feature fewer amenities, unless they are a custom conversion van.

B's will include a bathroom and kitchen, but with fewer amenities than larger rigs. You probably won't find an oven in B's and you might have a wet bath (meaning a combined shower and bathroom). And unlike A's and C's, Class B's generally will not have slide outs.

There will most likely be a bed, a couch that transforms into a bed or even a Murphy bed. Unlike Class A's and C's which typically have a private bedroom, B's are more open, like a studio apartment.

Oh, and in case I didn't mention it yet, all RVs—motorhomes, campers and trailers—built in the past few years come with flat-screen TVs. It is the 21st century after all.

Super C Motorhomes

So now you know what A's, C's, and B's are, and that they are named in a totally weird order. Just to make things crazy, let me teach you about Super C's.

Why Super?

A Super C is a Class C (same basic silhouette), BUT they have an 18-wheeler engine. Oh yeah. These big guys can haul. They are a great option if you're planning a lot of mountain travel, or if you want to tow a large vehicle behind your rig, like a truck.

According to my husband, these are the "sexiest" RVs. I don't want to know what that means. But if you're looking for a solid engine—and you can afford to pay top dollar for it—Super C is a great option.

Super C's will have all the amenities of a Class A or C, but because of their hefty price tag (you're paying for a diesel engine), they usually include extra features like washer/dryer hookups or a fake fireplace.

Buses and Motorcoaches

Photo credit: Technomadia

I'm going to avoid going into details on buses and motorcoaches for two reasons:

Buses: Most buses are projects. You buy an old bus and you have to build your rig yourself (or using a company). School bus conversions (skoolies) are becoming increasingly popular, but I know absolutely nothing about them. I do know that many RV parks will not allow skoolies to stay on site and it's rumored they are much harder to insure.

Want to customize your own RV? Buy an old bus. Check out a blog named Technomadia, if you want to see a really awesome bus conversion.

Motorcoaches: Are you a millionaire? Are you planning to open for Taylor Swift on her next tour? No? A motorcoach probably isn't right for you. They are huge, expensive, and difficult to maneuver. Plus, you'll have more money to spend on adventures if you don't invest it all in your coach.

Fifth Wheel Trailers

Photo Credit: Mandy Holesh, 188 Sq. Ft.

Average Length: 22 to 40 feet
Average Height: 12 feet to 13 feet 6 inches
Average Cost (new): $25K-$100K

Pros

- Amenities and layout most comparable to a house
- Largest kitchen option for any type of RV
- More privacy because bedrooms on opposite

sides of rig (available on most two-bedroom
layouts)
- Sleeps 4-8
- Price (more space for less money than
motorhome)

Cons

- Need to purchase a heavy-duty truck
- Outfitting truck bed for hitch
- Difficult of backing into RV sites, making u-
turns, backing up
- Designed for a slower pace of travel (compared
to motorhomes)
- Interior steps
- All of your travel will be in a truck (versus in a
"home", like with motorhomes)

Ah, fifth wheels. The first thing you should know: fifth
wheels are huge. HUGE. And as far as amenities go, I
think fifth wheels have the best options.

This type of trailer is called a fifth wheel because the
neck of the trailer (likely where your future bedroom is)
will sit in the bed of your truck, so the rig will be towed
from the bed of the truck instead of the hitch. Because
of this, fifth wheels have two levels (which means extra
stairs inside), so there is a little more privacy offered here.

In every fifth wheel I've seen there was: a fake fireplace,
a couch, possibly a second couch or two recliners, two A/
C units, a kitchen table with four chairs, an island, and a
fully stocked kitchen. This is the closest you will get to
living in a moving house and will offer the most space
and nicest amenities for the best price (generally speaking).

Heck, some fifth wheels have fold-out raised patios just because they are so fancy. Depending on how fancy you want to be, you can find a new fifth wheel for anywhere from 30K-100K.

I've been in a lot of RVs in the past two years and I must say, as far as interiors go, fifth wheels have the best design. While motorhomes still seem to be lacking in style, fifth wheels are aesthetically designed for a newer generation of RVers. I'm still waiting to find a rig that doesn't look like the fabric patterns were picked by a color-blind man, but new fifth wheels do have your least unattractive options.

Fivers are nice (if you have a truck to tow it with) because you don't have to worry about engine maintenance on the actual rig. Plus, when your truck has engine problems, you can take it to any shop, whereas most motorhomes can only be serviced at RV-specific or engine-specific mechanics.

When we were first buying an RV, people described fifth wheels like this — if you're going to stay in a place for a week or several weeks, fifth wheels are a great option. If you want a faster pace of travel, you should go with a motorhome.

Travel Trailers

Photo credit: Joe Hendricks

Average Length: 12 to 35 feet
Average Height: 10 to 12 feet
Average Cost (new): $12K-$45K

Pros

- Open floor plan
- Sleeps 1-8 (depending on the length of your trailer)
- Able to be towed on the hitch of your vehicle (compared to fifth wheels)
- Price (even cheaper than 5th wheels)
- Great for families (and typically a popular choice for families)

Cons

- Need to purchase a truck or large SUV for towing
- Difficult of backing into RV sites, making u-turns, backing up
- All of your travel will be in a truck (versus in a "home" like with motorhomes)

This is your classic pull-behind trailer. Of the options listed so far, this is the least expensive option. You have a great amount of space in travel trailers and you can expect the same amenities as a fifth wheel. However, because it is towed behind your vehicle, they are often shorter and smaller then fifth wheel trailers. In fact, you can buy trailers like Casitas or Scamps as short as 12 feet.

Kitchen, bathroom, dining area, bedroom—it has them all, but typically isn't as classy as a fifth wheel might be. In my own shopping experience, I've found that travel trailers have the most layout options for bunk beds and room for kids. One trailer even had a room with four bunks, in case you have a large family.

With any trailer, you'll need to own a truck and you'll need to start practicing backing up with a trailer. Many RV parks offer pull-thru RV sites, but more often than not, you'll need to back your trailer into its nightly home. If, like me, parking in reverse makes you sweat bullets, I wouldn't recommend a trailer if you're planning on fast-paced travel.

One of the biggest drawbacks to trailers of any kind is that on "drive days" you are stuck inside a truck all day. In our motorhome, I can stretch my legs, watch TV, work at the desk or kitchen table, nap in bed, make food, stare blankly into the fridge trying to find something to eat, and generally keep myself entertained while traveling. This is a huge plus for motorhomes if you ask me!

Truck Campers

Photo credit: Kelsey Henry

Average Floor Length: 6 to 12 feet
Average Height: 10 to 12 feet
Average Cost (new): $15K-$45K

Pros

- Easy to maneuver
- Lightweight
- Sleeps 2-3
- Designed to travel almost anywhere
- Designed for a faster-paced travel

Cons

- Fewer amenities
- Need to purchase a truck
- Need to outfit bed of truck to handle weight

- Some RV parks don't allow truck campers (these rigs are most often seen boondocking anyway)
- All of your travel will be in a truck (versus in a "home" like with motorhomes)

We decided against a truck camper when we realized it would actually be more expensive than buying a Class C motorhome with less than half of the living space.

Truck campers will be your shortest length option, unless you want to sleep in the backseat of your car. Will their small size, they can go just about anywhere.

Truck campers will have: a small kitchen (two-burner stove, sink, fridge), a dining room table that can double as a guest bed, a bathroom (which is most likely a wet bath, meaning you shower where the toilet and sink are), and a bed. If you don't mind occasionally waking up and hitting your head on the ceiling, a truck camper is a great option if you want to visit places off the map or fit down small roads.

Pop-Up Campers

Average Length: 10 to 27 feet (open or "popped")

Average Height: 8 to 9 feet (open)
Average Cost (new): $10K-$25K

Pros

- Easy to maneuver
- Lightweight
- Designed for travel anywhere
- Price

Cons

- Sleeps 1-2
- Some of them do not have A/C
- Few amenities
- No bathroom or shower

Don't live full-time in a pop-up camper.

Oops, sorry. There I go spouting my opinion.

My husband almost tricked me into a pop-up camper. Then I realized a HUGE deal breaker: no A/C (at least the one we were looking at).

Pop-ups usually do not have much kitchen space or a bathroom. Some will have a mini fridge and a sink, but that's not a guarantee! Overall, they are light-weight and easy to tow behind most SUVs, but I wouldn't recommend them for full-time travel unless you'll be in ideal climates or unless you really, and I mean really, like camping and the outdoors.

However, if you want to just weekend travel for a while, pop-ups are a fairly inexpensive option to test out the RV life without committing.

Teardrop Campers

Photo Credit: Brian Slaughter

Average Length: Less than 13 feet
Average Height: Less than 6 feet
Average Cost (new): $12K-$25K

Pros

- Easy to maneuver
- Lightweight
- Designed for weekend camping trips

Cons

- Sleeps 1-2
- No A/C (typically)
- Few amenities
- No indoor bathroom or shower
- Outdoor kitchen

Again, teardrops—like pop-ups—are not designed for full-timers. They are, however, super cute! Teardrops are becoming an increasingly popular option among RVers who want a retro camper-vibe. A typical Teardrop camper will have similar amenities to a popup camper, but less than a trailer.

I've never met anyone who lives full-time in a teardrop trailer. They are most often used by weekenders or part-timers who particularly love the outdoors. The good thing about a tiny rig like this is that you can take it virtually anywhere! (Plus, everyone will ask to check out your super cute tiny trailer.)

Picking Your Rig

At my current campground, I have three neighbors. All of them are married couples in their 50s.

One is in a 45′ Class A motorhome. Another in a 25′ Class C motorhome. And another in a 40′ fifth wheel. And they are all full-timers.

Everyone is different! Choose your RV based on what is best for you and don't let the choices of others influence your decision. We chose our rigs because motorhomes are best for the kind of travel we enjoy! But something different may be right for you.

Buying an RV is a mix of extreme excitement and stress to make the right decision. If you still have no idea what type of RV you want to buy, don't fret! I'll go over more considerations before making the big decision in the next chapter.

2

THE 3 BIGGEST FACTORS TO CONSIDER WHEN CHOOSING AN RV

Now that we've gone over what each rig is like, you've likely narrowed down your options based on your needs.

When we were shopping for our first RV, I was overwhelmed looking at motorhomes. Aside from knowing nothing about engines, how do you even know what a good length is for an RV? What's a good layout? And how exactly do slides work? They looked like just one more thing that could break to me.

These are some of the most important factors to consider before choosing your home on wheels. Let's break down length, slides, and height to help you make the best decision:

Length

Choosing the length of your rig depends on a lot of factors, but it boils down to two important details: weight and floor plan.

Weight

Weight is especially important if you're planning on purchasing a trailer or camper. You'll need to look closely at the towing capacity of your truck and the GVW (gross vehicle weight) of the rig.

If you're looking at motorhomes, this is less important—especially if you buy a diesel pusher.

But if you plan on towing a car behind your rig (we tow a Honda CR-V), you'll want to look at the towing capacity of the motorhome. If you don't want to tow at all and use a motorhome as your primary vehicle, you'll probably want to look at buying a smaller rig. (See Chapter 4 for more on towing)

Floor Plan

Weight is an important detail to note when deciding on your ideal length for an RV, but floor plan is typically the deciding factor for choosing length. Think about your must-haves in your rig. Maybe you know you 100% need an oven or two bathrooms or sleeping space for eight.

For us, we knew we wanted a floor plan that allowed two table tops for workspace, plus an oven and plenty of counter space in the kitchen. With only two people in our household, a rig between 30-35 feet would be ideal for us.

To get an idea of what length of rig you'll need, check out floor plans on manufacturer's websites. Many sites like Winnebago also offer virtual tours of their RVs so you can get a real feel for the space in each RV.

Slide-Outs

I mentioned slide outs, earlier but haven't explained what they are. Slide outs (sometimes called pop-outs or just slides) are portions of your RV that slide out when you're parked to increase living space. (If you're thinking "Alyssa, that's the stupidest definition I've ever heard", you're probably right. BUT I've had to explain slides to a lot of confused people who actually thought my RV was 12 feet wide when I drove it down the highway. Oy vey.)

Long story short: Slides are the best way to gain more living space. This is great if you want a shorter rig with ample space.

Slides are most commonly offered on class A's, C's, super C's, fifth wheels, and travel trailers. Slides can be electric or hydraulic, depending on the manufacturer. In a motorhome, you will still be able to walk around the RV with the slides in. This is typically not possible in fifth wheels and some trailers.

We have two slides: One that's about three feet deep and contains our dinette, and one that spans the entire length of the house and is about 18 inches deep.

These two opposing slides are fantastic for opening up the room and giving us a lot of floor space. I've seen very few other rigs with enough floor space to set up a stand-up desk and a yoga mat at the same time. If you prefer a more open concept RV, finding a rig with opposing slides is key.

You can expect to have issues with your slides at some point in your lifetime. They are known to be finicky, but the space is worth it. We've had issues with our slides on four occasions.

After purchasing our rig, we heard a few negative comments and reviews of full-length slides. We have had our large slide worked on three times in the past 18 months. In each instance, the slide was not coming in correctly. The front would come in faster than the back, or vice versa. Once the difference was so bad, our slide was out 6 inches in the back and not at all in the front. It was a nightmare!

The mechanic said this is called being "out of time." He re-timed the motors in the front and back of the slide so that they would start operating at the same speeds again. He said this happens often, especially with larger slides carrying a lot of weight.

My biggest slide tip: Unless you're buying a fifth wheel which is properly outfitted for excess weight, do NOT buy a rig with a refrigerator in the slide. I've heard horror stories.

Height

You have the least amount of control over the height of your RV. (I noted average heights for each type of rig in the first chapter for reference.)

Here's the deal with height: It is not a huge deal. Low clearances are rare, especially in the west and in the south. It likely will never affect visiting a specific destination, though it may alter your route.

Between All Stays, Co-Pilot, and our Rand McNally GPS, we never worry about running into low clearances. I recommend using at least one of these to check your route for clearances. Our Rand McNally GPS is built into our RV and our specs are programmed in, so we can trust it to never take us down roads we can't handle.

In three years of full-timing, we've only found ourselves in one terrible must-u-turn-now situation with low clearances. We were driving the I-95 from Connecticut to NYC and Heath took a wrong exit, one with about fifty WARNING: 8 FOOT CLEARANCE AHEAD signs. (He told me he saw none of them.)

A nice guy in a pickup flagged us down and said that if we wanted to keep our roof, we should follow him back to the interstate. We made it back on track in no time and I'm now a queen at backseat driving to make sure we never find ourselves in another heart-stopping situation like this!

3

WHERE TO BUY YOUR RV

You have a few options when it comes to buying your RV: a dealer, Craigslist, the side of the road, and in some cases you can even buy directly from the manufacturer.

People usually ask what is the best place for the best price (which is probably going to be the side of the road, those people are ready to sell!), but it all comes down to where you feel comfortable shopping. You'll find the lowest prices buying directly from a seller versus shopping at a dealership.

We bought our first RV through Craigslist. He took us to 48 states and only broke down once! Plus, we bought the 20-year-old rig for $11,500 and sold him 20K miles later for $9,750. He was the perfect first rig for us!

We bought our current rig from a dealer. Personally, I loved having a warranty for the peace of mind.

There are two big factors in deciding where to buy your RV: the year of the RV and finances.

Buying New

Obviously if you want something brand new, you'll need to visit a dealer or an RV show.

However, do NOT buy new.

I say this from experience, after I ignored the advice of full-timers before us.

Rigs "off the line" are often riddled with problems. I've heard this about every manufacturer, though some are better than others. Most full-timers I know recommend buying something at least two years old, as someone else has worked out the kinks at that point.

Armed with this knowledge, we expected a few visits for service, and we've made over a dozen in the past 18 months. It's been incredibly frustrating, especially when service departments aren't known for great service. (I'll talk more about servicing your RV in Part 4!)

Trust me, don't buy new! Plus, with the rapid depreciation of RVs and the steep cost, it's less of a financial burden to buy used.

Buying Used

You can find great deals on used RVs online—especially if you want a fixer upper and you're willing to take a small risk. Check out RVTrader.com. This is a great index of rigs across the country and you can filter results based on what you're looking for.

If you're worried about buying a used rig off Craigslist or from a private seller that might not pass inspection or might have leaks or other issues, you'd probably be most comfortable buying from a dealer. Dealers are required to put in enough maintenance to pass inspection before selling you the vehicle. This won't mean that it will be free of issues, but it will at least protect the basics. Plus you can likely get a warranty for a used rig using this method as well.

As far as price goes, dealers will generally be more expensive than private sellers. The best place to look for private sellers is Craigslist, but we've seen a lot of great deals on the side of the road or parked in neighborhoods too.

RV Shopping

As you search for the perfect rig, go RV shopping often. Attend local RV shows, visit local dealers, or even visit a local RV park to see what types of rigs are popular. This one of Heath's favorite dates for us and something we do often, even though we love our Winnebago!

Getting a Loan

Buying an RV is considered a luxury expense, which means it's difficult to find a loan. At 24 and self-employed, we really struggled to buy our Winnebago from a dealer. We used savings to buy our first RV from Craigslist, but we certainly hadn't saved up $125K to buy our Brave with cash.

This is where buying through a dealer can be an advantage. They will have access and information regarding best practices for securing an RV loan.

You cannot legally co-sign on an RV but you can do something called co-buying. (Literally the same thing, but with a legal loophole and a synonymous name.) If you want more details on co-buying, ask your banker or the finance manager at your local dealership.

4

11 THINGS YOU MUST KNOW BEFORE YOU BUY A USED RV

When we bought Franklin over three years ago, we were less than equipped to be RV shopping. In fact, before buying Franklin, we only looked at one other Class C motorhome. We bought the 20-year-old rig the same day we saw him—and that rig took us 20,000 miles across 48 states before we sold him to upgrade our RV.

He was a great purchase, but he wouldn't have been if we hadn't called Heath's grandpa every five minutes asking for RV advice. When given the chance, it's always best to hear advice from a fellow full-timer, someone who knows what it's like to live in a house on wheels and what parts of the RV need your attention.

Finding a good used RV can sometimes feel like searching for a needle in a haystack. Here are a few things to keep in mind when you're shopping:

1. Does the person showing you the RV actually own it?

First and foremost, make sure your contact is actually the owner of the RV. The first Class C motorhome we looked at was shown to us by the father of the man who owned the rig. He didn't have answers to our questions nor did he have any control over the cost of the RV. He wasn't able to tell us how it was stored (very important), how often it had been driven, or show us any of the maintenance records.

Unless the owner is deceased or you're buying from a used RV dealer, make sure you are able to ask the owner questions directly.

2. How many people have owned this RV, and how often have they driven it?

We were the fourth owners of Franklin. An older man bought him new, then a younger guy owned him for less than two years, then a family of four used it for regular camping trips. We purchased the rig from the family after they relocated from California to Texas.

Here's how we knew this was a good sign:

> 1. The rig had made it from California to Texas and was still running
> 2. The owners have kids, which meant they

would be more careful in maintaining a rig
trusted to drive their little ones

We didn't know much about the previous owners' use of
the RV, but we knew that at least recently, the RV was
kept up and used regularly.

Note: When buying a used RV, lower mileage isn't nec-
essarily a good thing. When someone is driving an RV
often, it usually means it's being well maintained. Lower
mileage when buying a used RV could mean it's been sitting on an empty lot somewhere and you can wind up
with a lot of issues.

3. Do they have maintenance records?

Maintenance records are the holy grail of buying a used
RV. We were instantly told that the transmission was
replaced in 2012 and that the cab of the RV sustained leak
damage and was fully replaced.

Every previous owner of the RV had meticulously doc-
umented all of the maintenance records. This showed us
that they were responsible enough to have things fixed (as
well as keep the records) and gave us confidence knowing
things were okay.

4. How many miles are on the tires and when were they last replaced?

If you obtain maintenance records from the previous
owner, you can probably learn this quite easily.

This is especially important if you're looking at buying
a used Class A RV. Class A rigs have extremely expensive
tires and replacing them is akin to college tuition.

Last summer, we noticed that due to an alignment issue

from the factory, our front two tires were wearing unevenly and needed to be replaced immediately. Fortunately this was all under warranty, because the bill came to a whopping $300/tire. Ugh. Check the tires carefully! This is less of an issue with Class C's, B's, or trailers that have similar tires to trucks, but still a large expense.

Even if you don't know much about tires, checking the tread is quite easy. Do they look worn out and have sun damage? If so, they probably don't have much life left in them. Do some research on how much it would cost to replace all necessary tires and then ask for that amount discounted from the price of the RV.

5. Check EVERYWHERE for water damage.

Inspect the roof and around all windows. Press on the walls and feel for soft spots that may indicate previous or continuous water damage. Water damage–in my opinion–is the number one reason not to buy a used RV. If an RV has water damage, save yourself now and do not buy it.

The reason? Often times it's hard to see exactly how bad the water damage is until you start digging into the wall. One little soft spot could actually be much more damage than you realize.

After buying our RV, we found a soft spot in the bottom left corner of a window, back behind the dining room chair. It was impossible to spot since the chair consistently blocked this area, but after a major rainstorm in Nebraska, we noticed a small puddle of water on the floor. This leak became a constant headache for us and a major lesson in properly sealing the RV. (We highly recommend all RVers travel with Eternabond tape, the sealant of the gods.)

6. Press all the buttons.

Turn on the engine (when applicable). Turn on every light. Check the clearance lights and brake lights outside. Turn on the generator (when applicable). Level the jacks. Turn on the hot water heater. Try the water pump. Turn on all the faucets. Test every feature to make sure they work. The last thing you want is to boondock one weekend and find out your water pump is broken.

7. Stand in the shower.

I'm actually serious on this one. I never showered in Franklin unless it was a necessity. The shower was way too small to be comfortable. Plus, my first shower experience was less than stellar and I hereby swore off the shower from then on.

Stand in the shower and see if you can handle it. While it may sound vain now, you'll be glad to have a rig with a good shower after three months out on the road, trust me.

8. Check under the unit for damage, rust, etc.

On Franklin, we (mostly Heath, ahem) scraped our back end on so many sloped driveways that we busted the metal wheels designed to keep your back end from dragging. The wheels were nothing but semi-circles when we sold our RV. While not a deal breaker for the buyer, be sure to take note of the undercarriage of the RV and how it's been taken care of. Look for rust, cracks, blatantly broken wheels, etc.

9. Ask what animals have lived in the RV and for how long.

Heath is very allergic to cats, so this is a must for us. You can usually pick up on this from smells, but it's imperative to ask if you have allergies. I also always ask about smokers, since I'm allergic to smoke.

10. Ask for a test drive.

Most owners will let you take the rig for a test drive. If they don't, do not buy it. Major red flag. Take the rig on open roads (especially if this is your first time driving an RV!) and gun it. See how the rig handles various speeds, how it handles turns, braking, swerving, etc.

Plus, see how you handle driving it. Does it feel much too big for you, or is it something you can adjust to? If you plan on taking the rig to national parks with mountains, take it up a few hills and listen to the engine (specific to motorhomes). Does it get too hot or whine in protest? Remember that the rig you test drive is likely empty and will be much heavier when it's carrying all your belongings, family, and full tanks.

Listen (or have whoever looks at the rig with you listen) for things that are rattling and moving while the rig moves. While not a deal breaker, this can be frustrating. I do know one couple who purchased a Thor and had an entire cabinet detach from the ceiling and crash to the ground while they were driving. So listening to these noises can be important!

11. Ask for an inspection.

Worth every penny–and likely less than $200. Ask the owner if you can have the rig professionally inspected before buying. We didn't buy a truck camper because we made this request and were vehemently denied. If the owner isn't hiding anything, they'll likely acquiesce.

This is good mostly for your peace of mind about buying a used RV. If your rig passes the third-party inspection, I'd say you're ready to start negotiating on the price!

5

TO TOW OR NOT TO TOW?

A tow vehicle—often called a toad, because RVers name things in weird ways—is a huge decision for RVers. Whether you're a truck towing a trailer or a motorhome towing a car, most travelers prefer or require a tow vehicle.

Towables

If you choose a trailer or camper, you'll buy a truck or a heavy-duty SUV. The size and model of the truck should be decided based on the size and weight of your rig. You can find all of this info in your owner's manuals. If you don't already own a truck, I recommend buying the RV first. That way you have more freedom to choose the right house for you instead of trying to find a rig that will specifically work with your truck.

Make sure your rig's GVWR (gross vehicle weight rating) doesn't exceed your truck's towing capacity. I wish it wasn't necessary to say this, as it should be common sense. But it's worth saying again. **Make sure your rig's GVWR doesn't exceed your truck's towing capacity.**

After picking your rig and your truck, you'll need to find the right hitch. You can find trailer hitches at your RV dealer or any auto parts store. If you choose a fifth wheel, you'll need to get your truck bed outfitted with a heavy-duty fifth wheel hitch. These are common and easy to find at any RV store or dealer. You can use sites like etrailers.com to find the right type of fifth wheel hitch for your specific truck.

Really, towing trailers and campers is simple. It's towing with motorhomes that gets complicated.

Motorhomes

With motorhomes, you have more towing options. With a Class B, you won't need to tow anything, since they are typically small enough to fit anywhere (and most likely their engines can't handle towing anyway).

But with Class C's and A's, it gets a little more gray.

If we do tow, should we get a tow dolly or tow four wheels down? If we tow four wheels down, what kind of tow package should we get? What's least expensive? What's safest? Should I tow a car behind my RV at all?

The past three years has been an extensive testing ground for all motorhome towing scenarios. Recently, we found what we believe is the best setup for our ideal form of travel: towing our Honda CR-V (automatic transmission) behind our Winnebago Brave "flat" or "four-on-the-floor."

Here is a scenic view of our current setup:

Before you make a decision on whether you should or shouldn't tow, I wanted to share a few of our towing experiences from the past two years.

Driving Without a Tow Vehicle or "Toad"

Our first year RVing, we drove our 1994 Class C motorhome to 48 states without a tow vehicle. This meant Heath drove our rig through cities like Austin, Los Angeles, New York City, Cleveland, San Francisco, and many others.

What We Liked About NOT Having a Tow Car:

- We saved a couple thousand dollars by not having to buy a tow package or tow dolly.

- Driving without a tow car was one less stress factor as a new RVer.
- We saved a few minutes of time when leaving campgrounds and arriving by not having to hook up a tow car.
- Better gas mileage.
- The ability to visit more places. For example, if we towed a car, we wouldn't have been able to take the Pacific Coast Highway all the way from LA to Portland because of the 30-foot limit.

The Downside of Not Towing a Car:

- If we wanted to visit major cities, we had to drive our RV into downtown areas.
- Trying to find a 29-foot parking spot was always stressful.
- Our RV was our only vehicle for errands. If we wanted to make a quick run to the grocery store, we had to pack everything up and move.

Conclusion: Driving a 29-foot RV through big cities is not fun.

Overall, the experience of driving our RV without a tow car was incredibly inconvenient. While it gave us one less thing to do when packing up our RV to leave a campsite, it also caused a lot of stress and limitations when we wanted do simple things like run to the grocery store because we ran out of milk.

Plus, if there were vehicle limitations for roads, we had to avoid those areas all together. For example, during our first trip to Glacier National Park we missed driving the famed Going to the Sun Road because there is a 24-foot limit. And in Big Bend, we couldn't visit a whole section of the park because of another 24-foot limit.

Driving Our RV With a Tow Dolly

A tow dolly is a trailer that allows you to tow with your front two wheels or all four wheels on top of a trailer. We used a tow dolly for only one day before we abandoned it in west Texas (long story), but we tried again a year later with slightly better luck.

What We Liked About the Tow Dolly:

- We finally had a vehicle to explore local areas, without having to bring the RV along.
- The tow dolly was free, since we were borrowing it from a family member. Tow dollies are quite expensive if you buy one new (and can be more expensive than a tow kit).

What We Didn't Like About the Tow Dolly:

- The straps on the tow dolly were a point of constant stress. They had to constantly be adjusted and would come loose during travel.
- It took a lot of time to hook up the car to the dolly.
- Driving the car onto the tow dolly trailer was a little unnerving. I never drove it off the front, but it's something we've seen many people accidentally do while using a tow dolly and it always terrified me.
- I was constantly worried about the car falling off the tow dolly.
- It was difficult to find a place to store the dolly if we stayed at a campground for more than a week.

Conclusion: Great having an extra vehicle, but the dolly was more stress than it was worth.

Overall, the largest benefit to having the tow dolly was having access to our car. However, the stress caused by the difficulty of hooking up and unhooking the car from the dolly was not worth it. If it hadn't been completely free to use, I wouldn't personally recommend one.

Towing Flat Behind Our Brave

Heath recently installed a Blue Ox Base Plate and Blue Ox Tow Bar so that we could tow our 2002 Honda CR-V behind our Brave. Instead of dealing with the stress of driving our RV through big cities or worry about messing around with a tow dolly, we have the comfort of towing our CR-V with four wheels down.

The past month and a half we've covered several thousand miles with our new towing setup. I wish we had done this from the very beginning. I was worried about the cost and difficulty of hooking up and unhooking the car from the RV. However, it takes just a few minutes to hook up our Honda CR-V behind our Brave.

What We Like About Flat Towing:

- It just takes a minute to hook up the car for towing (plus a couple minutes of running the engine).
- We have a much better turn radius while flat towing versus the dolly.
- I'm not worried about our car falling off the tow dolly and smashing into someone.
- It's less stressful knowing we have a Brake Buddy auxiliary braking system that will pump the brakes when we drive downhill and stop the car should it, for whatever reason, detach from the tow bar.

Conclusion: Towing flat behind the RV is our clear winner, because we can't think of any cons.

Towing our Honda CR-V with four wheels down has turned out to be the best set up. It takes just a few minutes before each drive to set everything up. Plus, the car follows nicely behind the motorhome and it's easy to forget it's even there (AKA it doesn't add more stress even though we're longer).

The manual in our CR-V gives us a simple set of directions and rules for towing which makes the process easy.

The rules are pretty easy. We aren't allowed to drive over 65 mph and before towing, we have to run the gears through a special sequence to lube the transmission. If we drive for more than eight hours in one day, which we never do, then we need to work through the sequence again.

How We Picked a Tow Package

Ultimately, there are two main companies who manufacture tow bars, Blue Ox and Roadmaster. After looking through multiple online forums that compared both companies, they both seemed like fairly even products. Some people preferred Blue Ox, some people preferred Roadmaster. There weren't a lot of differentiating factors with either tow bar as far as we could tell.

We went with Blue OX because we were on a time crunch and we found a local dealer who could get us all the parts in time.

Note: Neither company sells direct. You'll have to find a local dealer on their website or on Amazon. We chose Amazon because it's cheaper and we're all about Prime two-day shipping.

What We Had to Buy for Flat Towing

There were several different components we had to buy before setting up our Honda CR-V for flat towing.

Here's the list of big items we had to purchase:

A Blue Ox Alpha Tow Bar

This tow bar is rated to tow up to 6,500 lbs. and inserts into the trailer hitch on our RV. At the time of writing, this bar is on Amazon for $543.00, which is $150 less than local dealer prices.

A Blue Ox Base Plate

Note: base plates must be ordered specific to your vehicle's model and year. If you buy on Amazon, they have great filters for this.

We had to find a base plate that specifically fit the specs of my 2002 Honda CR-V. We couldn't find a seller on Amazon, so we ordered through a local dealer for this part and paid around $320.

Most dealerships charge several hundred dollars for this kind of installation, but luckily we had a friend who was willing to help guide Heath through the process. They spent three days drilling holes in the frame of our CR-V, removing our front bumper, watching YouTube videos for guidance and attaching the base plate.

Blue OX also sent step by step directions for installing this base plate onto the front of our CR-V which proved incredibly helpful. If you have a few days and don't mind a bit of manual labor, I recommend doing the install on your own.

A Blue Ox light kit

I'm sure any light kit would work. Just to make it easy, we ordered the Blue OX light kit to make sure that everything would work properly and it was around $45.

A Brake Buddy

An auxiliary braking system is designed to brake your vehicle for you as you tow it. Many states have towing laws that regulate whether or not you need some type of auxiliary braking system. You can find a complete state-by-state list of those regulations at brakebuddy.com/towing-laws. If you plan on traveling to Canada, it is required by law, hence why we bought one.

Brake Buddy, the most popular auxiliary braking system will run you around $1,000. It is extremely pricey, but definitely makes us feel more at peace and safer knowing that if something goes wrong, the Brake Buddy will take control of the car.

Before you buy anything...

This is a great time to read your car's manual. All cars can be towed in some capacity, and the manual will tell you the best way.

Most people, us included, prefer towing "four-on-the-floor." You must check your manual before trying this option. Not all vehicles can safely be towed four on the floor. A typical "tow kit" will cost at least $1,000. A tow kit will include a base plate and a tow bar.

If your car cannot be towed flat, you can tow any vehicle with a dolly (with 2 tires up) or on a flatbed trailer (all 4 tires up) depending on what the manual for your vehicle recommends. On average, a tow dolly or trailer will cost the same or more than installing a tow kit on your vehicle.

PART II

BEFORE YOUR
MAIDEN VOYAGE

6

ELECTRICITY
AND POWER

I'm not an electrician and I can't explain the ins and outs
of electricity in your rig...also that would be incredibly
boring. But I can tell you a little something about getting
power to your rig.

Shore Power

When you plug your RV into electricity at an RV park,
this is called shore power. (And yes, 99% of the time
you're camping at an RV park, you will have electric
hookups!) Odds are, your rig will pull 30 or 50 amps,
depending mostly on the number of A/C units on your
rig.

If you have two A/C units, you will have a 50 amp rig.
Typically this means smaller rigs like travel trailers and

Class C's pull 30 amps, while fifth wheels and Class A's pull 50. Some pop-ups and small trailers will only require 20 amps.

This information is vital because every single time you camp at a campground, they will ask. Many campgrounds divide their sites by what type of outlets are offered at each electrical post. So you'll need to be armed with this information.

So what if you get to an RV park and they are all out of 50 amp sites and that's what you need?

I recommend all RVers travel with electrical adapters. We carry an adapter and a 25-foot 30 amp extension cord that we use incredibly often. (You can see exactly what we use in the Resources section).

Should you find yourself camping at a friend's house or a Harvest Host's location or anywhere without the corresponding outlets, you can use adapters and extension cords to plug into to a normal 15 amp outlet. Sometimes this looks like a 50-to-30 adapter to a 30 amp extension cord to a 30-to-15 adapter. This isn't ideal, but it is possible if you really need electricity.

The most important thing to know if you are using adapters like is how many amps you are pulling. Our rig has a screen that tells us how much we are pulling and has a failsafe that will turn off outlets before we blow a breaker.

How many amps am I using?

- Microwave: 12-15 amps
- A/C: 7-15 amps per unit
- Space heater: 8-12 amps
- Refrigerator: 1 amp

- Lights: <1 amp, especially with LED lights
- Coffeepot: 8-10 amps
- Chargers for phones & computers: <1 amp

If you are worried about overloading, the best thing to do is to avoid running any heating or cooling systems and don't use the microwave.

If you are moochdocking[1] in someone's driveway or on a farm and really need to run the A/C for example, it would be best to crank on the generator to ensure you have plenty of power going to the rig.

Speaking of generators...

Additional Power Sources

If you buy a motorhome, there will likely be a generator built into your rig. If you buy a trailer, you will likely need to buy your own as an additional power source.

Why do you need additional power sources?

An additional power source is necessary if you plan on camping without electric hookups.

If you ever plan on staying at a national park campground or in the middle of the desert, you'll need an extra power source, like a generator or a solar set-up, to power your rig.

Generators for Motorhomes

Generators are the most common supplemental power source because they are built into most motorhomes and they are incredibly easy to use. In our Winnebago, we

---

1. This is where you camp on driveways or private land—usually owned by a friend, relative, or I don't know maybe you like staying with strangers—for free. You may or may not have electricity or water.

simply hold down a start button, conveniently located next to our refrigerator, and the generator will crank itself on.

Our generator can handle 46 amps, and it's likely that whatever generator is built into your rig can handle the same amount of pull as shore power. If you're looking for a power source that can easily run your microwave or your A/C units, this is your best option.

In motorhomes, the generator will likely be connected to your fuel line. So if you have a gas rig, your generator will pull gas from your tank. If you have a diesel pusher, it will pull diesel from your tank.

In this case, there is a failsafe in the generator that will turn itself off if your fuel level dips below 1/4 of a tank. That way you don't run out of gas and end up stranded anywhere.

Generators for Trailers and Campers

Since your rig likely won't come equipped with a generator, you'll need to consider if purchasing one is necessary. (I'll outline two additional power sources below as options.)

Typically a new generator will run about $1,000 and you'll need to carry additional gasoline (or diesel or propane, depending on the generator) for fuel. Propane generators are becoming increasingly popular, but gas generators are the most common.

The con for generators is the carbon footprint. You will be burning gas and creating toxic fumes. The only time our carbon monoxide detector has ever gone off was when we left the windows open while our generator was running. (Yep, don't do that!) Environmentally speaking, this isn't the best option. But it will provide you with the most power and because of how little gas it uses, it can be the most economical option.

Batteries & Inverters

Underneath our couch are three heavy-duty RV and marine deep cycle batteries that connect to an inverter that powers our rig.

While we are driving, our house batteries[2] and inverter will run our fridge and our outlets. This means I can charge my phone or laptop, watch TV, or even straighten my hair...not that I've ever done that while Heath is driving...

An inverter is great for supporting this type of usage. While it can shoulder the heavy pull of our coffee maker or the microwave, it will zap a lot of your available amps and wear down the batteries.

Without the inverter in our Winnebago, there would be no power to our rig while we are driving or boondocking. In our first RV, we would need to crank on the generator even for small tasks like charging our laptops for an hour.

The additional batteries and the inverter mean we can use all of our outlets at any time.

Plus, since our Winnebago is equipped with a residential fridge instead of a two-way or three-way powered RV fridge[3], the inverter is necessary. Without it, we would

2. Motorhomes have at least two batteries: *coach*, for the engine, and *house*, mostly used to feed power to the lights, refrigerator, generator, and furnace.

3. A two-way or three-way fridge are the types of refrigerators most commonly found in RVs. They are smaller than a residential fridge, but can be powered by propane, shore power, or 12V power (aka your house battery).

constantly need to run the generator or be plugged into power.

However, an inverter is not a reliable long-term power source. Our batteries can last overnight before needing to be recharged. Our batteries recharge in three ways: running the engine, running the generator, or plugging into shore power.

I haven't been thrilled with our battery bank, perhaps mostly due to user error. We have three RV-Marine batteries hooked up to our inverter. We didn't know how to properly take care of our batteries and ended up shortening their lifespan. (Apparently, you don't need to add water to the new RV marine batteries, like everyone suggests.) They lasted less than two years and at $200 per battery, they were expensive to replace.

It's important to never let your batteries die and never let them get too low. In this way, you need a generator, shore power, or even solar to help keep your batteries from ever dying.

Based on the cost of the batteries + the inverter + the work to install them into an RV if it isn't built in, I would never add this to my RV as the main power source. We use our inverter any day that we are driving and when we boondock, but it doesn't provide enough power to handle more than our fridge and our lights. You can always add more batteries, but they are expensive and take up space.

Solar

We live in the age where solar for RVs is becoming more and more common. More and more rigs are becoming "solar ready," which I think is just the manufacturer's way of saying that you can add solar to the rig if you want to, but they aren't going to shoulder that expense. I know that Winnebago has started installing solar on their Class B and C rigs, but I haven't seen it on many trailers or bigger motorhomes yet. But hey, progress!

A solar set up can be costly, usually upwards of $1,500, and depending on the part of the country, it may not even be useful.

In fact, after telling friends that we planned on spending time on the east coast in the mountains, they advised us against solar, because large trees will block our power source. (Plus there are less public lands for boondocking on the east coast, but we'll get more into that in Part 4.)

Based on what we've learned from other RVers, I would invest in solar only if you plan on boondocking often and if you're planning on keeping your RV for an extended period of time (long enough to get the value after the upfront investment). If we would've known when we bought our Winnebago that we would travel in it for two years, I would've made the investment for solar.

The best part about solar is that you never have to worry about gas or recharging. The sun is always taking care of you. You will then, of course, always be searching for camping that isn't shaded. However, if you're looking for the most environmentally-friendly option, this is it!

7

JACKS & THE ELUSIVE LEVEL CAMPING SITE

It took two months of sometimes waking up with splitting headaches before we realized we were making a terrible mistake: We weren't leveling our RV properly. We were sleeping with our heads just slightly below our feet and it was wreaking havoc with our health!

If you've lived in a house your whole life, you've likely never worried about this! But making sure your RV is level is vital.

Modern large RVs are equipped with leveling jacks. Your jacks may be hydraulic or electric depending on the make of your RV. Jacks are helpful for a number of reasons:

1. Many RV parks do not have level sites. This is a con-

stant headache for RVers, literally. From experience, if you sleep with your rig unlevel and your head is below your feet while sleeping, you'll wake up with a wicked hangover. Jacks will save you from this horror.

2. Jacks keep your RV more stable, so it doesn't rock as much as you're moving around (or, ya know, *moving around*).

3. Jacks can help save your tires, by relieving pressure on them when you're parked.

Jacks in every rig are a little different, so you'll need to consult the manual or the previous owner to learn how to operate them. Our first rig had two buttons and joystick to control the jacks. Our current rig has a big button that says "Autolevel" and it is amazing. Many trailers will have manual jacks and smaller RVs may not have jacks at all.

You will want to level your RV every time you park overnight and anytime you pop out your slides.

In addition to your jacks, it's a good idea to carry leveling blocks that you can place under the jacks or under the tires. We once had our jacks slip on a gravel site and our RV came crashing back down to the ground. Okay, it only fell like 1/2 an inch, but it felt scarier.

Leveling blocks will also help you when you get stuck with a particularly unlevel site. Say, for example, you level your RV with your jacks and you notice your front two tires are off the ground. This is not good. It means two things: You've likely fully extended your front two jacks and they are bearing the full weight of the rig (bad!), instead of distributing the weight across the jacks and the tires.

If you level your RV and find that any of your tires are off the ground, pull up the jacks, add leveling blocks under the necessary tires and re-level your jacks. Bringing your tires off the ground will add unnecessary strain to the jacks and is a recipe for disaster.

Some RVers will chock the wheels after leveling their rig, but this isn't necessary for motorhomes the way it is for trailers.

If you buy a smaller or older RV that isn't equipped with jacks, leveling blocks under the tires will help level your rig. We use Lynx leveling blocks, which are basically adult Legos, for leveling and they're extremely sturdy. Some old school RVers use 2x4s or blocks of wood instead.

Why you should always level your RV

In 2014, we parked our RV on a driveway that was slightly slanted while we stayed in a friend's house. We didn't lower our jacks since we were housesitting and didn't want to scuff their driveway with our metal jacks. So our RV was unlevel for a few nights while we enjoyed endless hot water.

And our propane fridge...DIED.

Check the fine print, many propane refrigerators have a 3° margin between normal operation and catastrophe.

When unlevel, the flow of chemicals behind the fridge is disrupted causing them to mix improperly and likely creating a nasty chemical reaction. A tiny explosion of chemicals, no big deal!

It wasn't pretty back there, trust me.

If you are unlevel, make sure you switch the fridge to run off electrical or battery power and not propane to prevent this. If you run into this same issue and blow up the back of your fridge, there is one, simple, possible solution: it's called burping. Actually, if your propane fridge ever stops working, this is a likely solution.

Remove your fridge and turn it upside down on its head. Let it sit for 24 hours. This will help the fridge redistribute the chemicals properly. Then flip it back over and hook it up. Wait a couple hours and check to see if the unit is cooling again.

Flipping the fridge isn't easy and it's definitely a two-man job. Really. Cause I tried to help Heath and I totally dropped my side. He asked some guys at the RV park for help.

Our burp didn't work, likely because we didn't try this solution until a full week after our incident. So definitely try this right away if you want to save your fridge. Or just park on level ground!

8

TANKS: NO ONE'S GOING TO DUMP THEM FOR YOU

You have four major tanks in your rig: fresh, grey, black, and propane. I'll explain propane first, since it's the simplest.

Propane Tank

Your propane tank powers your furnace, stove, hot water heater, and likely your fridge (unless your rig has a residential fridge).

As full-timers, we refill our propane tank every 3-4 months for roughly $50. (If we were to stay in wintry locations, we'd burn through propane faster. But we don't do that, because why would you be in an RV and intentionally visit the cold?)

Your propane tank is most likely underneath your rig and will be the one door in your storage bays that will not lock, for safety purposes. Trailers will store propane tanks often on the tongue of the trailer.

Only certified people can fill propane tanks, which can make fueling up on this gas difficult. Some RV parks offer propane on site, but we most often fill up at truck stops or large gas stations.

If you plan on being parked in one place for an extended period of time, many RV parks have a "propane guy." For some reason, this is how all RV parks refer to this person. But this propane guy will drive to your site and fill up your tank from a tank on his truck. This can be an expensive service if you call them yourself, so ask the RV park where you are staying if they offer this. Many parks will have their propane guy come by once or twice a month for this service.

For safety, any time your propane tank is being filled, all living beings need to step outside of the RV.

Propane Safety

People are often worried about propane in their RV. There is a lot of fearmongering and horror stories that get passed around online, but I encourage you to not be intimidated! Propane is no more dangerous than gasoline and is used in most RVs.

Most fears are centered around visiting gas stations. You do NOT have to turn off your propane tank when fueling up your RV. While it is recommended that you do not use propane while fueling (i.e. using your stove, furnace, or hot water heater), you do not have to turn off your entire tank.

Some people are concerned about even running their fridge on propane while driving or while fueling up. We have never turned off the propane to our fridge while driving or while fueling up (and I don't know of anyone who does this!).

As an added safety measure, all RVs are equipped with propane detectors as well as carbon monoxide detectors so you don't have to worry about gas leaks either. (Ask me to tell you sometime about the time Heath accidentally broke our propane gas line. Ah, death-defying times.)

Fresh Water Holding Tank

Your fresh water tank holds your clean water. The key word here is hold. You'll only use water from this tank if you are NOT hooked up to water at a campsite, but instead using water you've stored onboard.

Your rig will come equipped with a water pump, which will pump water from your tank to your faucets. This is what you'll use for washing your hands, showering, everything. Generally, it isn't recommended that you drink this water, depending on the age of your holding tank and how long the water has been stored.

You'll use water from this tank on drive days or when you're dry camping.

We try to never fill our fresh water tank all the way, because of the sheer weight of water. Driving with a full tank will lower your gas mileage and make towing more difficult. For us, a full tank weighs 483 lbs.

On drive days, we typically fill up our tank less than 1/

4 full so we have enough water to boondock overnight if necessary. A full tank of water will last us an entire week—if we don't shower.

Grey Tank

Your grey tank collects all the water that drains from your sinks and shower. This tank will be roughly the same size as your fresh water tank.

Your grey, since it contains a mixture of soapy water, dirt, and food scraps that make it through your drain, rarely smells, but can sometimes leave a sweaty odor. You'll want to dump your grey tank every couple days while traveling, remembering to always dump your grey after your black.

If you're parked in your RV for days or weeks at a time, you can leave this tank open to prevent flooding.

A short story about flooding:

Should you go too long without dumping your tanks, the grey water will come up through the lowest drain, typically your shower. How do I know this? HOW DO I KNOW THIS?!

Experience.

Fortunately, Heath did this when I was not in the RV. But still, ew.

Dump your tanks regularly and monitor your levels.

Black Tank (Or your septic tank)

Your black tank contains waste only from your toilet(s).

You will need to always have toilet deodorant handy, because this is the stinky tank. Toilet deodorant (which you can find in the RV section at Walmart) will neutralize the odors in the tank and help disintegrate toilet paper.

To keep your black tank from clogging, use septic safe toilet paper. Cheap store brands or Angel Soft work well. Dump your black tank regularly to prevent odor, and after closing your black tank, add deodorant. This is typically when the smell is at its worst.

As I said before, always dump your black tank first and your grey tank second. In that way, your grey tank will flush out anything your black tank may have left in the sewer line.

Never under any circumstances leave your grey and black tanks open at the same time. This will cause the tanks to mix, which would be catastrophic.

How to Unclog Your Toilet

The culprit to most toilet clogs is your toilet paper. If you frequently have issues with this, switch your toilet paper brand to something that will better disintegrate. Or maybe see a doctor, I don't know.

Unclogging an RV toilet can be pretty simple: Boil a pot (or 2, or 3) of hot water and pour it down your drain. This will break down the toilet paper and help clear the drain. Hold your breath while doing this folks, so as to not pass out from the foul stench it unleashes.

If this doesn't work, toss some baking soda and vinegar into the toilet bowl and flush it down, then pour the boiling water down the drain.

To prevent clogs in the future, make sure you use septic safe toilet paper, don't use too much of it, and flush plenty of water down the drain after each use.

9

QUICK, COMMON SENSE DRIVING TIPS

If you haven't driven an RV around before, your first time behind the wheel for a big road trip is going to be scary-exhilarating. Here's a couple things to remember to keep you safe out there:

Take it slow

You're wider, heavier, and longer than most vehicles on the road. Expect most cars to pass you, even 18-wheelers.

Slow down, let others pass you, and remember you're driving your house. Max speed when towing will be listed in your manual. 65 mph is the standard max speed. Be sure to find this number in your truck or tow car manual and obey it. Please take this to heart! I see far too many RVers flying down the road at unsafe speeds.

Besides, you're out driving to take in the views and explore someplace new. There's no need to speed.

Take wide turns

Consider the length of your RV and your wheelbase. Pay extra attention if you're towing a car behind you.

Watch out for dips and steep parking lot entrances

More than once—okay, more than a hundred times—we've scraped the backend of our RV trying to drive in and out of parking lots. Gas stations, Walmarts, grocery stores—they are not all RV friendly! Be sure to look at the incline of the parking lot entrances before turning in.

Many rigs have extra support wheels in the back to help prevent this, but we actually broke ours off from too many of these mistakes. Learn from us!

Read all road signs

My husband is admittedly terrible at this. Keep your eyes out for construction signs and detours. But most importantly watch for low clearances and narrow roads. Many GPSes will route you to avoid these areas, but it's still important to watch for signs. We'll talk more in chapter 17 about choosing the right GPS.

Turn your clocks to RV time

Your rig—regardless of what you purchase—will not and should not get you places at the same speeds as your car. RVs are slower and your detours at gas stations and rest stops will take a little longer.

When we type our destination into the GPS, we always add time to the ETA for this reason. Our general rule is that you should add 15 minutes for every hour of Google Maps drive time. We call this "RV Time".

This means if Google Maps says you're four hours away, expect to take at least five hours to get there.

Knowing how slow (or relatively slow) you will be traveling your RV is helpful for setting expectations on the road. Expect to pull over for meals at scenic overlooks, or to stop in cute small towns along your route, or to refuel and stretch your legs. This is the beauty of RV travel! You can take it slow and stop as often as you want.

Take a driving class

Depending on the size of your RV, you may want to take a driving class! I'm sure you're an excellent driver, but these classes are great for giving you peace of mind on the road.

There are many options for classes. You can ask your local dealer for a recommendation, or check with national companies like RVschool.com or RVsafety.com. If you don't want to take an in-person class, there are free video lessons on Youtube as well.

At the end of the day, you're driving your house down the road at 65 mph. You want to feel comfortable!

10

PACKING YOUR RV

Let's make this RV feel homey! You're probably moving out of what we full-timers call a "sticks-n-bricks", AKA a building with walls and a foundation. You will have to store, sell, donate, or trash a lot of your belongings. I know, it's hard. But it's worth it.

When Heath first moved into our RV, he filled every cabinet on his own. This was after selling, donating, and taking stuff back to his parents' house.

Then he remembered he still had a wife to move in (and that she would be supplying everything for the kitchen). He had to take out all of his belongings and cut the pile in half. This is typical for most people moving into an RV. You own more than you think and you need less than you think.

Downsizing can be a long, emotional process for many people.

To make your life easier, I've included a packing list based on two people. This will help you trim the fat of what you do and don't need.

Kitchen

Utensils

- Pot with lid (1)
- Skillets (1 large, 1 small)
- 9×13 cake pan
- Pizza pan (Standard cookie sheet will likely be too large for an RV oven)
- Bread pan/Casserole dish
- Mixing bowls (2)
- Colander
- Cutting board
- Spatulas (2)
- Mixing spoons (2)
- Tongs (2)
- Whisk
- Set of measuring cups and spoons (1)
- Can opener
- Pizza cutter
- Peeler
- Wine/bottle opener
- Wine stopper
- Basic silverware set for eight
- Oven mitts (2)
- Food storage clips (4)
- Plates (6)
- Bowls (6)

- Coffee mugs (4)
- Travel tumblers (4)
- Cups (8)
- Reusable water bottles (2)
- Tupperware, assorted sizes (12)
- Ziploc bags – sandwich and gallon size

Cleaning Supplies

- Dish rack
- Paper towel holder
- Paper towels (2)
- Dish soap
- Dish brush
- Sponge
- Kitchen towels (8)
- Flyswatter

Appliances

- Coffee maker (We use an espresso machine and a French press for when we don't have electric hook ups)
- Blender
- Toaster
- Slow cooker or InstaPot

Staples

- Basic spices (Salt, garlic, cumin, etc.)
- Oil
- Vinegar
- Baking Soda
- Sugar

- Coffee
- Tea
- Etc, etc, based on your family's dietary preferences.

Bathroom

The Basics

- Shampoo (1)[1]
- Conditioner (1)
- Body wash (his and hers)
- Lotion
- Hair spray
- Washcloths (4)
- Towels (6)
- Beach towels (2)
- Baby wipes
- Shaving cream
- Razor(s)
- Tooth brushes
- Toothpaste
- First aid kit
- Hair dryer
- Cotton balls and cotton swabs
- Hand soap
- Sunscreen

Cleaning Supplies

- Toilet cleaner (septic safe)
- Toilet deodorizer

1. If you don't plan on showering in your RV, I recommend two sets of shampoo and conditioner, one for each spouse when using bathhouses.

- All-purpose cleaner
- Trash can
- Toilet brush

Living/Dining Room

Entertainment/Hobbies

- Books[2]
- Movies (packed in a CD case)
- Extra cords (USB, iPhone, etc.)
- Atlas
- Atomic clock
- Suitcases (2)[3]

Basic Office Supplies

- Envelopes
- Thank you cards
- Printer paper
- Spiral notebook
- Tape (masking, duct, scotch)
- Pens
- Dry erase markers
- Scissors
- Headphones
- Hard drives

Important Records

- Passports

---

2. We carry some physical books, but rely primarily on our Kindles.
3. We store our suitcases under our booth. Under the bed is another good option.

- Tax files
- Insurance paperwork
- Vehicle registration
- Maintenance records

Bedroom

- Bedding
- Pillows
- Throw blankets (2)
- Mattress topper, RV mattresses are seriously bad
- Backpack/laptop bag (2)
- Duffel bag
- Clothing
- Battery powered fan (for boondocking)
- Space heater

What NOT to Pack

You should know what clothes and essentials you'll need based on your current closet. Based on my years of experience, here's what you really don't need:

- More than one coat
- More than one sweatshirt
- More than one suit
- More than one nice dress
- More than one pair of high heels
- More than two purses
- More than two swimsuits

Under storage

- Drinking water hose (50 ft)
- Sewer hoses (3, assorted lengths)
- Sewage Tracks
- 30 AMP extension cord
- 50/30 AMP adapter
- Toolbox
- Extra screwdrivers
- Tire pressure gauge
- Extra fuses
- Spare tire
- Folding chairs (4)
- Leveling blocks for your jacks
- Water shoes

Required for Extra Fun:

- Bicycles
- Kayaks, inflatable for easy storage
- Grill
- Hammock
- A good camera

11

HOW MUCH DOES RVING COST?

People frequently shrink away from conversations about money and finances. I've never quite understood this, considering that after almost 20 years of schooling, I never encountered a single class on financial literacy or loans or how many arms-and-legs worth of dollars you'll waste on rent after college.

When Heath and I moved into our RV, we had no clue how much campsites would cost, how high our Verizon bill for internet would get, or just how many thousands of dollars it would take to visit all 50 states.

We moved into an RV because we wanted to travel across the country for our honeymoon, but we've continued to full-time RV because it's a cheaper, more freeing way to live. In fact, over a million Americans full-time RV. That's crazy!

So exactly how much does it cost to live in an RV? Let's break it down:

The Rig

RVs aren't cheap. Well, new ones aren't at least.

We bought our 1994 Coachmen Leprechaun in 2014 and sold him 48 states and 22,000 miles later. After buying and renovating "Franklin" for $12,000 and selling him for almost $10,000, we really only spent $2,000 for our home for two years. (I'll get to lodging costs in a minute!)

This is the definition of a steal and probably the main reason why I highly recommend buying used. We lived in Franklin full-time for 18 months before upgrading to our new RV. If you're worried about buying a used rig off of Craigslist, I can tell you that we only broke down once when in 20,000 miles. So I'm very pro-Craigslist purchases.

Our 2016 Winnebago Brave (MSRP $123,000) required a $10,000 down payment, which selling Franklin covered for us. We pay $600 a month for our RV, which is fairly high considering what I've heard from others who have bought new RVs. Most people I know who are financing rigs pay between $400-$600 a month.

Gas

After your RV payment, gas can be your biggest expense on the road. It is also the expense you can control the easiest, by traveling less or traveling shorter distances.

In three years of travel, our most expensive month of

gas rang up to a whopping $1,200, which is when we traveled through California when prices soared to $4/gallon in 2014. It was terrible.

We average $2,000-$4,000 per year in gas (that is for our two car and motorhome combined). Our Honda gets 20-25 mpg and our Winnebago gets more like 7-9 mpg.

Overall, we spend less in gas each month than we expect to. Expect a few hundred dollars a month, depending on how many miles you're covering.

Lodging, Rent, and Campsite Costs

We spend an average of $400/month on camping fees. That's roughly $13 a night.

Since I've stayed in RVs parks in 48 out of 50 states (not in Hawaii, obviously, and not in North Dakota because there was absolutely no good reason to stay in North Dakota a minute longer), I can tell you that most RV parks average $35-$45 a night. We've seen RV sites for over $100 during our trip to the Florida Keys (but our site had a private beach, so 100% worth it!). And as I'm writing this paragraph, we are at a riverfront campground with full hook-ups for only $25 a night, which is one of the best-valued campgrounds I've ever seen.

To save on lodging costs at RV parks and campgrounds, you can always opt for fewer hook-ups. When we want to save a couple dollars, we will choose electric and water only sites and use the dump station when we leave the park.

I'll talk more in Part 4 about ways to save money, alternative camping options, and how to find the best places to camp.

Grocery Costs

This number will stay roughly the same as what you spend wherever you're living now. We spend up to $400 a month in groceries for our family of two. We buy mostly fresh foods and shop 1-2 times a week since there is limited cabinet space in RVs.

Other Food Costs (Restaurants, Fast Food, etc.)

I do not eat out often. If it were up to Heath, we'd eat out every day. Probably for breakfast. He is a sucker for pancakes and since I am gluten-free, we almost never have pancakes in the house.

Anyway, we average about $100 a month in eating out, which is mostly restaurants and Starbucks, not any fast food. From people that I've talked to, this is extremely low. Many full-time travelers are super into trying local restaurants when they travel, so they obviously spend a lot more on restaurants. But if you're moving into an RV to downsize, pay off debt, or build wealth, you're in control of spending as little eating out as you want. If you're moving into an RV because you want the full experience of all the places you visit, you'll drop a few hundred on eating out each month. It's your call.

Phone & Internet

We pay roughly $300/month total for unlimited data on our phones (through Verizon) and on our hot spot (through a black market AT&T plan). I'll get into the details on choosing internet and phone providers in chapters 15 and 16.

Maintenance

Always, always, always expect to incur maintenance charges each month. Expecting to pay each month for maintenance will save you many headaches and knots in your stomach when you inevitably break down, blow a tire, shatter a brake pad, or have a propane leak—all of which have happened to us. You'll need to be changing your oil and refilling on propane regularly anyway, so it's best to just count this as a guaranteed expense.

Our biggest maintenance occurred when our fuel pump gave up just south of the Grand Canyon. We paid $600 to get it replaced and get back on the road. We are probably pretty lucky that our biggest maintenance expense was that low, but I'll take it!

We typically spend around $1,000 in maintenance annually. Based on our experience over the past three years, I'd save $100 a month for this so you are prepared when bigger fixes arise.

RV Insurance

This number can vary wildly depending on your rig. Nicer rigs like diesel motorhomes will be more expensive. Incredibly popular and inexpensive rigs like travel trailers will be cheaper to insure.

For our 1994 Coachmen RV, we paid between $600-$700 a year for RV insurance.

For our 2016 Winnebago Brave, we pay just shy of $2000 a year for RV insurance. And for the record, my husband is the guy who is on the phone with the insurance agent always saying, "Oh yeah, I want that covered. An extra $200 dollars? Sure no problem!" We are ridiculously over-insured, I'm sure.

Our car insurance is closer to $500 a year since we pay for the lowest possible package and have an old car. Plus, our RV insurance should also cover our tow car in case of an accident. I say "should" since insurance companies have terrible reputations for telling you things that aren't true.

We found our car + RV insurance through Good Sam, which connected us with National General and Allied, respectively.

Health Insurance

I cannot give you an estimation of cost for your health insurance. It changes too rapidly and is too subjective! I will say that we pay $249/month currently for both Heath and I. I'll get more into the details of how to find health insurance for RVers in chapter 13.

So what's the monthly total?

Those will be all of your big-ticket expenses. There are always other random expenses: Spotify, Netflix, taxes, fees, movies, books, clothes. But you're completely in control of how much you'll spend on those categories.

The Rig: $600 (or less!)
Gas: $250
Lodging: $400
Groceries: $400
Eating Out: $100
Phone/Internet: $300
Maintenance: $100
RV Insurance: $2000 for the year, or probably $150 a month
Health Insurance: $250

Total: $2,550

That's living comfortably. In our '94 rig, we paid as low as $1,400 one month. If you don't finance an RV like we currently are, you can save a lot of money while traveling.

PART III

TRANSITIONING INTO RV LIFE

12

RV INSURANCE

The first thing you'll need to do after buying your rig is to buy RV insurance and register your vehicle. This can be tricky! Vehicle registration and insurance MUST be in your state of residency. (I'll talk more about establishing your residency, or domicile, in chapter 8.)

If you've been alive for any period of time, you know that insurance can be a real pain in the neck and that is especially true when it comes to RVs. Here's the most important thing to know: **Not all insurance companies will cover full-time RVers.**

If you plan on full-timing in your RV, you need to explicitly say this to your insurance agent. I do believe the insurance definition of full-timing is spending more than six months of the year in your RV (but this could change at any given time).

To make things more complicated, it is not uncommon for an insurance company to tell you they do not offer full-timer insurance, when you know for certain that they do. (I'm looking at you, Progressive.)

We decided to go through Good Sam[1] to find our insurance. They made the process much easier for newbies like us, since they will look at multiple insurance companies and give you options.

Our current policy is through Allied Insurance. We've used them for three years and they've been great.

People often worry about what happens when your RV is in the shop and you suddenly don't have a place to sleep. While most mechanics will let you stay in your RV overnight, many full-timer insurance plans have an allowance for hotel nights for this purpose. We've used this once when we broke down just south of the Grand Canyon.

Allied reimbursed us for the hotel quickly and easily. I love the peace of mind knowing that if we end up homeless for a night, we will still be able to find a place to sleep.

One thing you will definitely need on the road as part of your insurance package is roadside assistance. I would not travel without it.

We've used Good Sam's Roadside Assistance. It costs less than $100/year and they really saved us when we had a tire blowout on our tow dolly in middle-of-nowhere California. They blew us out of the water with their customer service and they went above and beyond to help us find the right tire.

---

1. Good Sam doesn't seem to have a great reputation among RVers, but we've had nothing but good experiences with them. They do not pay us to say nice things about them...but they should.

13

HEALTHCARE OPTIONS FOR RVERS

Ah, healthcare. This is probably my least favorite subject to talk about. It invites so much controversy, confusion, and rip-your-hair-out hassle. Not to mention finding healthcare for RVers is ten times more complicated than it is for sticks-n-bricks people.

We've been RVing for three years and have tried quite a few options for coverage on the road. We've actually used something different every year because until this year, we have not been happy with our options.

When you're rarely in your home state or domicile state, it's hard to find healthcare coverage that will take care of you when you're off exploring Denali National Park.

In this chapter, I'll talk about our own experience with insurance on the road.

Note: I'm no expert in healthcare because let's be real, the rules change too much for anyone to be an expert. This is purely our own experiences. If you're looking for medical advice, you've come to the wrong place.

2014: Obamacare/Affordable Care Act

Before Heath and I were married in 2014, I was on Obamacare and Heath was on his parent's insurance plan. (It's worth noting that after we were married, Heath stayed on his parent's insurance plan until his 26th birthday last year.)

At the time, I was paying $4.87/month for health coverage with Blue Cross Blue Shield. I had a terrible catastrophic plan with a super high deductible.

Of course, if anything happened to me, this type of plan wouldn't provide much financial support, plus I had zero idea if I was covered country-wide. Definitely do not recommend.

2015: No Healthcare

Despite making very little our first year on the road, we did not qualify for Affordable Healthcare in 2015. I imagine this was mostly because we are self-employed. Since we didn't receive any government subsidies and because our business was just getting started, we couldn't afford to shell out $200/month or more for health insurance, period.

All of the plans we looked at were over $200 to insure just me. At 24 and self-employed while also paying down student debt, there was no chance we could swing that.

Choosing to not sign up for healthcare was a huge point of stress for us, but financially it was our only option.

Since we were young and in good health, we felt dropping our coverage wasn't too big a risk and we did our best to not get me pregnant.

We did have to pay the 1% of our income penalty for not having insurance, but this was still significantly less than how much it would've cost to insure me for the year. I, however, do not recommend this course of action.

2016: RVers Insurance

In 2016 we signed up for my health insurance through RVers Insurance Exchange.

Signing up with RVer Insurance was a little complicated and confusing, but offered a lot of peace of mind since they specialize in finding health insurance coverage for RVers and up until this point, we were researching health plans ourselves.

We called and talked to Colleen, explained our situation, and told her what we were looking for. We filled out some forms—which we had to print out, fill out by hand, and then fax back to them like it's 1987—and she called us back the next day with multiple options.

Colleen found me a plan that would cover me across all of America with Scott and White Health Plan. It was a whopping $265 a month for just me. Talk about a kick to the gut. And that was the cheapest plan she found for me.

If you are looking for traditional health insurance, I HIGHLY recommend going through the agents at RVer Insurance so you can be sure you're finding a plan that will allow you to access healthcare wherever you are traveling. This is the #1 concern for RVers. You want to make sure your insurance will cover you nationwide! They also offer options for telemedicine, which can be a great if you can't find a doctor wherever you are in your travels.

2017: Liberty Healthshare

Earlier this year we signed up for Liberty Healthshare as our healthcare provider. It is easily my favorite option for RVers so far because it is infinitely more affordable.

Liberty Healthshare isn't health insurance, it's a health care sharing ministry.

If you haven't heard of healthsharing, let the internet explain what it is.

"A health care sharing ministry is an organization that facilitates sharing of health care costs among individual members, in the United States, who have common ethical or religious beliefs." (Wikipedia)

If your first thought is "Huh?" let me put it layman's terms.

Instead of paying an insurance company each month, you pay other people's medical bills. And when you make a claim, instead of an insurance company paying the claim, other people in your healthsharing community pay for your bills.

This means a few things:

- You're working with a 501(c)3 non-profit, not an insurance company.
- You can actually see where your money is going, because it goes toward individuals. (Liberty automatically charges my credit card each

month, but online I can see that last month our
money went to David & Elizabeth.)

- You don't have to worry about finding a specific
  provider when looking for care.
- It's significantly cheaper than insurance.
- It is exempt under ACA requirements, so you do
  not have to pay a penalty.

I would be skeptical about joining a healthshare ministry,
but before signing up we talked to several people who
have used healthsharing and raved about it (including my
parents).

My parents, fellow entrepreneurs, joined Samaritan
Ministries after the Affordable Healthcare Act passed,
making traditional healthcare unaffordable for them.
This is a pain point for many of our self-employed
friends. My family has claimed several procedures and
doctors visits over the years and have had nothing but
good things to say.

We would've joined Samaritan years ago, however, you
are required to have a pastor's signature and sign a statement of faith. It's hard to have a "home church" when
you're never in a place longer than a month, so we were
unable to join. (Remember the foundation of healthsharing is that you share medical costs with a group of individuals with common ethical or religious beliefs.)

This year, we chose Liberty Healthshare. Liberty is reli-
giously affiliated like all healthsharing organizations, but
does not require you to be religious. You do sign a statement of good faith that basically says I'm a good person
and uphold the aforementioned common ethical beliefs.

I asked my friend, Michelle, who I knew used Liberty
Healthshare for advice on signing up. After hearing her

rave review, she passed my information onto her contact at Liberty.

They called me (the call was less than three minutes), emailed over a few forms I could fill out online, and we were done!

Plus, since everything is internal (versus calling RVers Insurance and them looking around at all other providers for plans), we looked at the chart on their website and picked our plan in 5.2 seconds.

Since we are under 30, we pay $249 for coverage for Heath and me. That's $16 less than health insurance for just me in 2016 AND the coverage is better.

Honestly, this was a no-brainer for us. And while we, of course, hope to never have to file claims for medical expenses, I feel confident that Liberty will take care of us.

If you want to go through RVer Insurance to have an agent help you find a plan that's right for you, they now offer healthsharing plans in addition to other insurances.

Finding coverage across the country from an insurance company you can trust is extremely difficult right now. Based on our experience in the past few years, I recommend Liberty Healthshare for getting the best coverage for your money.

However, you should do your own research, call RVers Insurance if you have specific questions, and always choose what is best for your specific situation. That, and take a deep breath and don't let finding health insurance stress you out too much!

Prescriptions

Your cost and access to prescription medicine will depend on what insurance option you choose.

People often worry that traveling will prohibit basic healthcare tasks, like fulfilling prescriptions. However, in today's world this is relatively simple to remedy. Pharmacies at Walgreens, Walmart, and CVS provide country-wide access to pharmaceutical care.

We don't rely on prescriptions on the road, but in our research have found that Walgreens is known for having the best nationwide service and offers great flexibility with changing your pickup location.

14

GETTING MAIL AND ESTABLISHING YOUR DOMICILE

The first question people ask when they learn I live in an RV is always incredibly boring: "How do you get your mail?"

Mail can be especially tricky if you'll be full-timing, and there are few different options. First things first, you'll need a permanent address and that means establishing your domicile.

Why you need to establish your domicile

In the US, you need a permanent address for everything—RV parks will even ask for this info!—which is difficult when you live on wheels and no longer have a "permanent residence". Having a permanent address is necessary for registration, voting, insurance, taxes (and so on and so forth), which is why you'll need to set up a domicile before you hit the road.

Your domicile is essentially your new home address and there are three key states that make great domiciles: Texas, South Dakota, and Florida.

Picking your domicile state

If you're already from one of these three RV friendly states, then you're lucky! That's how we ended up choosing Texas.

But the state you choose is totally up to you! Since laws are different from state-to-state, here are a few of the main factors to consider when picking your state:

- Taxes (Income, sales, vehicle, etc.)
- Vehicle inspection and registration laws
- Homeschooling laws (if you have kids on the road!)
- Driver's license renewals
- Jury duty
- Where you plan to travel

Where you plan to travel is important if the state you choose requires annual visits. We have to visit Texas every year to update our vehicle inspection. This isn't a big deal since we visit our families at least once a year, but it can be a hassle depending on where you plan on traveling.

A lawyer told me that when picking your domicile,

what you really are doing is crafting your story. Maybe your story is that you decided to move to South Dakota until they finally finish the Crazy Horse monument, or maybe you're snow birding in Florida like all the retirees. Your story is simply a way to tie you back to your new home state.

This story is important in a few instances, like when you get pulled over by the cops for example. I had a cop pull me over earlier this year for a brake light being out in my car. After looking at my ID, he asked why I was in town. I told him I was on my way to a film shoot. Because I was so far from home, he advised me that it's illegal to have an out-of-date address on my ID and that I needed to update my address in the next 30 days.

Sigh. This is why your story is important. There's nothing illegal about establishing your domicile and traveling full-time. Knowing your story (and the law) is key!

So, how do you actually establish your domicile?

There are services that will set up your domicile for you. Our favorite is Escapees because they can set you up in any of the three states, and they do a lot more than just mail forwarding. St Brendan's Isle is highly recommended for Florida and My Dakota Address for South Dakota.

Escapees will establish a domicile for you, give you a permanent mailing address, and even forward your mail to you on the road (while filtering out the junk!). Once you find a service that you like, getting your mail on the road is extremely easy.

Once your address is set up, you'll get to go through the super fun process of changing your address on everything. Driver's license, bank accounts, bills, insurance, etc.

I highly recommend going through a service, because they can easily walk you through all these steps.

Receiving packages on the road

Amazon Prime is the best invention of the decade and an RVer's best friend. We often have packages sent to RV parks, and with two-day shipping guaranteed, we've never had any issues!

If you're trying to receive any type of package on the road, the easiest way to do so is to ship it to the RV park where you are staying. We usually let the campground know ahead of time that we are expecting a package. They will accept the mail for you and call you when it's in (in our experience).

This is incredibly common and easy. Just make sure your address label looks something like this:

Name of Campground
Attn: Alyssa Padgett Site #52
Address
City, ST Zip

Including your name is important for both USPS and the campground receiving your package. Don't forget this step!

If you're boondocking or not staying in a campground, you can have your package shipped to the post office or a UPS store. I had to pay $5 to pick up a box from the UPS store while we were camping in the Tetons. The fee is annoying, but it's a good option if you don't have a physical address to ship to.

If you choose to ship to a post office, you'll want to send your mail "general delivery." Or like this:

Alyssa Padgett
General Delivery
City, ST Zip

I personally prefer to send all mail and packages directly to our campground so there's less of a chance it gets lost in the shuffle. Like I said before, we use Amazon frequently on the road and so far (knock on wood) we've never had a package get lost or miss us on the road.

15

INTERNET ON
THE ROAD

If you're planning on working on the road, your first thought is probably how in the heck am I going to get internet?

Relax everyone, most RV parks have wifi and 85% of the time, it's free. And if you don't mind waiting 10 minutes for your email to load, RV park wifi will treat you just fine.

But if like most people, you want/need/can't live without the Internet, you'll need to buy an unlimited cell plan for internet access.

We've used two unlimited cell plans in our time RVing: Verizon and AT&T.

Let's start with Verizon.

With Verizon, we used a Verizon Jetpack (This jetpack does not allow you to fly through the air. This jetpack is a mobile hotspot that creates an internet connection for you). We used our jetpack for two years.

We loved Verizon because they have great coverage across the country. The only places we didn't have coverage: west Texas and remote parts of national parks.

We ran our entire business on this device, streaming video calls with clients, recording podcasts, uploading videos to YouTube, etc. It handled everything like a pro.

Now Verizon is known for being pricey and if you get a plan through them, you'll pay monthly for data. And it will be incredibly expensive...unless you find an unlimited plan.

Initially, we paid out of pocket for 20 GBs of monthly data and we still spent a lot of time in coffee shops because of our data limit. Along with our two phones, this was $220/month.

So, Heath and I went to the black market to snag ourselves an unlimited data plan. Looking back, I have no idea how we survived working our first year on the road without it.

With our unlimited plan, we can work freely without worrying about using all our data or needing to go to a coffee shop to download files. Plus, we can stream YouTube, Netflix, and podcasts easily. Which sometimes means way less productivity in the Padgett RV, but also meant we could start our YouTube channel and Heath could continue his podcast.

Our unlimited Verizon plan cost $140/month.

These black market unlimited plans can be hard to find. They are available on eBay, but joining a community focused on internet like RV Mobile Internet will ensure you have reliable coverage. I have friends who bought on eBay and their hotspot was shut down! To avoid wasting money or going through that hassle, take the time to find a solid bootleg plan.

If you're looking to connect with someone who can give you an unlimited plan, send me a message at HeathandAlyssa.com and I can connect you. I know that sounds sketchy, but I have to protect my provider!

Now on to AT&T.

We just started our AT&T plan in May of 2017 when Verizon cracked down on unlimited plans. Losing our Verizon plan was heartbreaking, especially since Verizon has way better countrywide coverage than AT&T.

But we are traveling on the east coast this year, and AT&T has better coverage on the east coast anyway, so we made the switch without too much fanfare. (We do still use Verizon as our cell provider.)

We still have a bootleg plan, from the same guy who supplied our Verizon plan, and it's been good so far…and by good so far I mean we've streamed Netflix basically every day and we've watched a LOT of YouTube videos with ease.

We use the Unite Explore AC815S device. It cost us $140 for the device (one-time) and $100 monthly for unlimited data. (Our Verizon plan had cost us $140 monthly for unlimited data.) I don't remember how much we had purchased our jetpack for, but the price is comparable to AT&T.

Having used both, I would say that Verizon is definitely better and is worth the cost if you rely on internet while traveling. If you choose either of these two options for internet on the road, you will be fine. I would not travel full-time without an unlimited internet plan like what we have now. We couldn't run our business!

One way to make sure that you always have service is

to invest in a cell booster. A cell booster has the ability to heavily boost your cell signal while camping in remote areas. Really since many RV parks are off the beaten path, we use our cell booster at 75% of the places we camp. WeBoost is the brand of booster we use and they make units specifically for RVs. The booster and antenna will cost about $500 in equipment and will take a few hours to set up. (We have a video showing our install process on our YouTube channel.)

While it's a fairly hefty upfront investment, setting up our cell booster has effectively eliminated our stress about losing cell signal. We know are always covered.

RV Park Wi-Fi

Once in South Dakota, Heath and I extended our stay at an RV park for three extra days because they had *real* wifi. I could instantly load a page and everything! We celebrated by streaming Gladiator on Netflix.

Most RV parks do have internet, but if you're planning on working on the road, do not rely on this. You can likely check your email and maybe your Facebook. But it won't lend itself to much more.

We use a Winegard wifi ranger that is designed to help boost your signal connection, but since most RV park wifi isn't very strong to begin with, we haven't relied on this. Your best chance at reliable internet connection will be an unlimited cell plan.

16

CHOOSING YOUR CELL PROVIDER

You probably own a cell phone. (If you don't, how do you survive?!)

You probably have had the same plan for a few years, but you don't know if that same plan will support you on the road as well as it does in your hometown.

A lot of RVers I know use T-mobile because it's typically your cheapest option for a cell phone plan. But (and this is a huge but) those are the people who complain about not getting good coverage. T-mobile is great for out of the country use—in case you're headed to Canada or Mexico—but notoriously bad in the states.

What's more important: saving money or being able to

call roadside assistance when you're on the side of the interstate?

I'm in favor of paying more for better service. If you're planning on full-time RV travel, I recommend Verizon or AT&T. And I highly recommend using the opposite service of whichever you choose for internet. Then you have really good chances of always having signal.

We've used Verizon for our phones for nearly four years with no complaints. I switched from Sprint, which offered me signal basically nowhere, but they like T-mobile have much cheaper options.

Personal observation: 80% of RVers I meet use Verizon, especially those who work on the road.

17

THE RIGHT
TYPE OF GPS

One of my most popular blogs of all time included a huge fight between me and Heath and our dreaded GPS.

It was all caught on camera, and in retrospect, it was completely ridiculous and NOT AT ALL MY FAULT that the GPS suggested two consecutive u-turns.

Most GPS units won't know that you're driving your house down the road, which can make navigation frustrating. You'll need a special GPS, one designed for truckers or RVs.

Our Winnebago came with a built-in Rand McNally GPS that has our specs integrated into it, so it knows to avoid low clearances and small roads. If you buy a brand new motorhome, you'll likely have a GPS included. If not, Camping World and RV dealers will have multiple GPS options for you to consider.

However, since it's 2017, many of us prefer using our phone as a GPS.

We recently started using CoPilot, an app that downloads all North American maps to your phone so that it doesn't need data or cell service to operate.

It costs roughly $50 for the app and will take up 2 GBs of space on your phone. If you're planning on visiting remote places without cell service or want to make sure you always have map access, this is a great option.

If you're not into paying for a specialty GPS, you can always use Google Maps on your phone for free, which is updated regularly and is a good option. Just pay close attention to watch for low clearances and weight limits on roads, since Google maps will not warn you about these!

Even if you do buy an RV or trucker GPS, you should 100% buy an atlas. We've used ours multiple times, mostly in situations where construction, low bridges, or tunnels have ruined our travel plans. It was a lifesaver when we tried to navigate the George Washington Bridge out of Manhattan and something we always keep on hand.

PART IV

LIFE ON THE ROAD

18

RV CLUBS AND MEMBERSHIPS

Before we started RVing, I didn't know RV memberships were a thing. Really, I didn't know full-time RVing before retirement was a thing.

We jumped into full-timing with little knowledge or experience in the RV world. Our goal was not to be RVers. Our goal was to visit all fifty states. Turns out, buying an RV was the most affordable way to make this happen. And so we bought a fixer upper off of Craigslist, planned our route, and took off four days after our wedding.

Because it took us so long to pack up the RV and hit the road on that first day, we knew we wouldn't end up arriving at a campground until after camp offices closed at five pm. Instantly we were faced with an unforeseen problem:

How do you check into a campground if there is no one there?

Before we left Texas to head west, we joined only one RV membership at the suggestion of a friend: Passport America. We had no idea how to use it or how it all worked.

I found a campground near our destination using Passport America's app and gave them a call. The woman in the office told me to find any open site and set up camp for the night. She said to drop by in the morning after the office opened and pay for our stay. We were shocked by this for a few reasons:

She wasn't worried at all about us not paying.

She accepted our Passport America discount (50% off) without asking for a member number.

This campground with wifi, a heated pool, and a hot tub cost $19.

Instantly, I fell in love with Passport America. (Really I'll fall in love with any campground that offers a hot tub).

I'm all about saving money on the road, so RV memberships are high on my list of things worth paying for each year. In this post, I'll break down the most popular five RV memberships, their benefits, how much they cost, and if I think they are worth it.

The Top Five RV Memberships (based on popularity)

- Good Sam
- Passport America
- Escapees
- Thousand Trails
- Harvest Hosts

Good Sam Club

Good Sam Club is Good Sam's reward program (a separate fee from their insurance, roadside assistance, and any other services).

Cost

- $27 annually
- $50 for two years
- $69 for three years

Benefits

- 10% off camping fees at participating campgrounds
- Over 2,100 participating campgrounds
- Up to 30% savings at Camping World
- 3¢ off the gallon at Pilot and Flying J

The Problem with Good Sam

Good Sam is one of those companies people love to talk crap about. This is especially true with RV park owners. As a user, I'm grateful that most RV parks right off the highway are part of Good Sam. The discount isn't much, but having the little Good Sam icon on their RV park makes me more likely to choose that park over other nearby campgrounds.

However, here's what I've heard from park owners: RV park owners pay thousands of dollars to be listed on Good Sam Club's website and in their phone book of listings. Not even for big ads promoting the park, just to have their name as part of the database. That's RIDICU-

LOUS amounts of money parks are conned into paying–especially since most RVers do not go to GoodSam-Club.com/travel/campgroundsandrvparks to search for a place to stay.

Here's where it gets worse: GS assigns a three-part ranking to every participating park. It rates the facilities, the restrooms, and the appeal. After talking to multiple RV park owners, these numbers directly correlate to how much the RV park pays Good Sam for advertising.

Take the ratings at a recent park we visited, for example:

GOOD SAM RATING (?)

Facility	Restrooms	Appeal
9	9.5★	9.5

RVer REVIEWS

★★⯪☆☆

View All Reviews   Write a Review

Good Sam says this park should be super awesome, but the reviews by actual RVers are terrible. Basically, Good Sam is the Yelp of the RV world.

Oh, my other problem with Good Sam: they send you mail. Like, a TON of mail. All of which are trying to upsell you on their other services–even services you already use. They send me mail at least once a week trying to sell me products of theirs that I already own and trying to convince me to buy more. SO ANNOYING.

Is Good Sam Club worth it?

If the average price of an RV park is $35, you save $3.50 per night with Good Sam. This means you'll need to use your GS membership discount for at least a week of camping to make back your investment before you actually start saving money.

We used our Good Sam discount for less than ten nights this past summer–most notably for a week-long stay at Nugget RV Park. While we loved this particular RV park and have stayed here twice after leaving Glacier National Park, when it comes to saving money on the road, Good Sam isn't a great investment.

We've used Good Sam for nearly three years and I highly doubt it's saved us more than $50 in that time frame. The 10% discount isn't enough to make a huge difference. (However, I definitely recommend Good Sam's Roadside Assistance which has saved us hundreds of dollars.)

Passport America

Passport America is the 50% Discount Camping Club.

Cost

- $44 annually
- $79 for two years
- $109 for three years

Benefits

- 50% off camping fees at participating campgrounds

- Nearly 2,000 participating campgrounds
- Easy-to-use mobile app
- Affiliate referral program

The Problem with Passport America

Passport America parks have a reputation for not being very nice. We've definitely stayed at some trashy $12 parking lots that call themselves RV parks. However, we've also stayed at a bunch of RV resorts with pools, hot tubs, good wifi, game rooms, and all the perks that come with resort RV parks. The good thing about Passport America is that you can really easily view amenities. You cannot, however, see real reviews like you can with Good Sam.

Here's Passport America's webpage for Valencia Travel Village, the RV park where we always stay when we visit LA:

Valencia Travel Village

27946 Henry Mayo Rd (Hwy 126)
Castaic, CA 91384
US
No Toll Free Number
Local: (661) 257-3333

Normal Price(s): $55.00 *
PA rate(s): $27.50 *

Join Now and Start Saving!

Valencia Travel Village Amenities

Cable TV

Clubhouse

Dump
Station

Golf

Handicap
Access

Heated
Pool

Hot Tub

Ice

Partial
Hookups

Playground

Pool

Propane

Pull-Thrus

Recycling

Restrooms

Security

Showers

Shuffleboard

Store

Tennis
Courts

I can easily see on their website (or on their app) that this park has a pool, hot tub, golf, tennis, a playground, and more. They even offer security, so I know this will be nicer than most RV parks out there. If you pay attention to these icons, you can get a good idea of what an RV park will be like before you arrive.

But again, PA does not have any reviews or any way to directly read real customer reviews to give you a better sense of what the RV park is like.

Is Passport America worth it?

Passport America pays for itself in two nights, or even with one use if you use it in California where it pays for itself pretty much instantly. Hands down, every single RVer should join Passport America. We've saved hundreds of dollars over the past 2+ years because of PA.

But you shouldn't just join Passport America to save money. PA is also a great way to make money on the road.

Passport America offers $10 affiliate commissions for all referrals. So, if you use my link to sign up for Passport America, I earn $10 for referring you. For Heath and I, this is a great way for us to promote a product we use constantly and also make a little extra cash. Plus, if you sign up a campground for Passport America, you can earn up to $100 for the referral (but Heath and I have never done this). Anyone who uses PA can have their own affiliate link, so you can make money this way too!

Escapees

Escapees RV Club is a support network for RVers.

Cost

- $39.95/annually
- $850 for lifetime

Benefits

- Support network with answers to basic RVer questions
- Travel guides
- Job center for finding work on the road

- Mail service & domicile options (additional fee)
- Rallies

The Problem with Escapees

I joined Escapees thinking that it was another RV park discount program. They do have some RV parks that offer Escapees members discounts, but Escapees is more about community and life on the road than about saving money.

If you're looking for another discount program, this is not the place to look. Here's what their website says: There are nineteen Escapees parks located from Washington State to Florida with unique options and nearly 1,000 commercial RV parks that offer a 15-50% discount.

However, I couldn't easily find a place where these RV parks are listed and found this confusing.

Is Escapees worth it?

Finding community and connecting to other RVers on the road is not easy. We are often asked how to meet other RVers and how to combat loneliness on the road.

Escapees offers meet-ups and rallies all across the country as a way to help connect RVers. There are 11 rallies being hosted this month alone.

Plus, they have hundreds of articles and videos on their website to answer all of your RV-related questions—which is great for new RVers. This is especially helpful when it comes to needing quick maintenance advice you can trust.

If you are new to RVing, Escapees is a great membership for helping you learn more about the ins and outs of RVing and connect with other full-timers.

Plus, they also have "Xscapers" for younguns like Heath and I. If you're a "young" RVer (basically if you're under 50, you're young) then this is another great way to meet RVers who are not retirees. No offense retirees, but it's nice to meet working-age RVers too.

Thousand Trails

Thousand Trails offers a slightly different kind of membership club. For a larger upfront fee, you can camp without charge for up to 14 or 30 days at a time (depending on the level of membership you purchase) at participating Thousand Trails campgrounds.

Cost

- "$545 annually" (Quotation marks here because Thousand Trails pricing plans are more confusing than American healthcare)

Benefits

- 86 campgrounds in five "zones" across the country
- "Free" camping in your selected zone

The Problem with Thousand Trails

I rarely hear anything good about Thousand Trails. I've heard they can be confusing and difficult, with horrible customer service. Not to mention that they are pricey, come with hefty restrictions, and the parks themselves aren't very well kept.

We recently met a few members of the PR team at

Equity Lifestyle Properties, the company who owns Thousand Trails and Encore Resorts. They let us know they are in the process of renovating and updating many of their parks to make them better destinations.

We visited three of their parks during our recent visit to the Florida Keys and they were all amazing. Hopefully this means that the brand is improving as a whole and will be a better deal for RVers in the future.

Is Thousand Trails worth it?

Probably not. The idea behind Thousand Trails is awesome. You pay an annual fee, you can stay at their locations for free all year, you save thousands of dollars on lodging and save time researching campgrounds.

It sounds like a great way to save money, and if the company was more well-run, then it might be. However, I do not recommend buying Thousand Trails, just based on the current reviews. The poor service isn't worth it.

If you do want to try Thousand Trails, buy a used membership on eBay instead of paying full-price through Thousand Trails.

Harvest Hosts

Harvest Hosts is a unique RV membership that allows campers to park their RV for free (for one night) at select wineries, vineyards, breweries, farms, and museums.

Cost

- $40 annually

Benefits

- One free night of camping
- Good way to meet locals
- 500+ locations

The Problem with Harvest Hosts

When you're parking at HH sites, you likely won't have hookups of any kind. Plus, in accordance with Harvest Hosts setup, participating business owners typically will only allow you to stay for one night.

However, I know from lots of friends that the nicer you are (and the more wine, beer, etc. you buy), the more likely it is that you'll be allowed to stay longer, especially during the week or during off-season.

Is Harvest Hosts worth it?

YES. In one night, Harvest Hosts theoretically pays for itself.

However, the idea behind HH is that you camp for free (saving yourself at least $35) in exchange for purchasing products. Since most participating HH businesses are wineries or breweries, this is a great way to immerse yourself in the local area and try local flavors. But buying a couple bottles of wine will *easily* run you more than the cost of a campsite.

For just saving money, this isn't the best membership. Your lodging costs will go down, but your spending will likely go up.

For meeting people, exploring a local area, and having a good night of food and drink, HH is amazing!!! (They deserve all the exclamations points, they are so wonderful!) We recently spent three nights at multiple HH stops on the east coast. We spent over $100 buying a wine tasting, a few bottles of local wine, and dinner. This is more than we would've wanted to spend in lodging, but we met great people and had a lot of fun, so it's worth the cost in my book!

19

HANDLING RV MAINTENANCE

Whether you live in a house, an apartment, or a home on wheels, maintenance is part of life. Stuff breaks.

This is a huge point of stress for RVers. When you need a simple oil change, you temporarily lose your house. In this chapter, I want to share our experience with maintenance and how it will affect living full-time in your RV.

Heath and I have always chosen to live in motorhomes—first a Class C, then a Class A. We've loved both of our rigs and highly recommend choosing a motorhome when people ask us which rig to buy.

But after suggesting buying a motorhome, people come back with this unexpected question: **But where do you sleep when your motorhome is in the shop?** What do you do when your house goes to the mechanic?

While it's true that the engine in the motorhome will land you in the mechanic's shop more often than a trailer would, chances are, if you travel long enough, you'll end up stuck at the mechanic at least once. I'll get to where you sleep when your motorhome is in the shop in a second, but first a story.

My friends Joe and Rhonda travel full-time in a beautiful Airstream. A couple years back, they were traveling through the Napa Valley when they started having issues with their floor.

They went to an Airstream mechanic and learned they needed to get their entire floor replaced. This meant everything had to be moved out of their RV. Their personal belongings, the cabinets, the appliances, EVERYTHING.

This is the worst-case scenario for RVers. In one day they lost their whole house and were given an estimated six weeks of repair time. Yikes!

Because Joe and Rhonda are smart creative people, they found a local winery with a small cottage on site that they could rent for the time their trailer was in the shop. They actually "work-camped" for the winery, trading Joe's photography services for rent, in order to afford to stay in such an expensive part of the country.

Now that's one extreme example of what may happen with your RV on the road. Most of your maintenance issues will be much less complicated and, fingers crossed, less expensive. The longest we've been forced out of our RV is a few hours, and mechanics are extremely accommodating to full-timers.

I say all this to say:

- Towable or motorhome, it doesn't matter. At

some point, you might temporarily lose your house for maintenance.

- You can always find a place to stay, no matter how crazy your maintenance issue is. Don't let this fear ruin your RVing future!

Where do you sleep when your RV is in the shop?

1. Stay in your RV!

99% of the time your RV is in the shop, the mechanics will let you stay in your RV overnight. Many RV dealers have sites with electric posts for this very reason! We have done this often, including when we had our RV serviced at Winnebago's manufacturing headquarters. Some dealers and manufacturers will have full RV parks with hookups where you can stay while waiting for service. This is always the cheapest and most convenient housing option.

2. Use your insurance.

We had to do this on our 10th day of full-timing when our fuel pump gave out in the middle of nowhere Arizona. It was June, 100+ degrees outside, and we pulled up to the mechanic at 4:30 PM on a Friday night. The perfect storm, really.

The kind mechanic, realizing our plight, told us he couldn't get us on our way until Saturday morning, but offered to let us stay the night. He plugged us into their power (only 15 AMP) in their bay, so we could run our fan and refrigerator. However, the Arizona heat bested us and forced us to look for better accommodations.

Most full-time RV insurance will include a stipend for

hotel stays when your RV is being serviced. If your mechanic doesn't have a place for you to camp or you cannot stay overnight in your RV for any reason, this can be a "free" option for the night. Our RV insurance through Allied would reimburse us for up to $500 spent in lodging while our RV was in the shop. This is common among many RV insurance providers and something I highly recommend adding to your policy.

We walked to a local hotel, found a room for $120, and paid with our credit card. We submit a receipt from the hotel along with the receipt from the mechanic to our insurance company. They reimbursed us within two weeks and we ended up enjoying endless hot water and central A/C for the night.

For only a few extra bucks on our insurance bill, this insurance feature paid for itself in one night. Dealing with your insurance company may be a hassle, but the luxury of enjoying a night in a hotel coupled with knowing you have a place to stay if your home breaks down is totally worth it.

3. Call a mobile mechanic.

Mobile mechanics sound so convenient! And they are–if they can actually fix your problem. From our experience and what we've heard from others, they are helpful about 50% of the time. If your troubles leave you stranded somewhere, this is likely your best option, so you can avoid the costs of being towed to a mechanic.

We've used mobile mechanics twice: once with our first RV, when our tow dolly blew a tire and needed replacing, and once when our slide was stuck half-in, half-out.

In the first case, we had amazing service and someone

had a tire out to us in a couple hours, even though we were a hundred miles from the closest tire shop.

In the second case, the mechanic showed up, told us that he couldn't solve the problem, and handed us a bill.

Sigh.

We actually ended up driving down the interstate to a mechanic shop with our slide sticking out six inches because we had no other way to fix it!

Mobile mechanics are great for small fixes that don't require many parts, or fixes that leave you stranded and unable to get to a mechanic. Hiring mobile mechanics will also allow you to stay in your RV while it is being worked on, however, you've got about a 50/50 shot they can really fix your problem.

4. Plan your service appointments ahead of time.

Sometimes you blow a tire and need service immediately. But in many cases, you have a few small things that need fixing that all add up. This is especially true if you have a new RV with a warranty. (Remember: This is another reason why we don't recommend buying new!)

We like to plan our service appointments ahead of time so we can set up alternative lodging options. This has looked like taking our RV to the mechanic over the holidays, when we are out of town for work, or when we go on vacation.

This has worked well for us in the past, especially when we are called out of town for work. However, this plan recently failed us…

The only place we will service our RV now

Before our warranty was up on our Winnebago, we tried

to schedule an appointment with our dealer to get our rig serviced.

We had a long list of fairly minor fixes. Things like getting the cables replaced on our captain's chairs because they snapped, which made reaching the gas pedal frustrating and difficult. Plus we had a piece of our countertop that was slowly breaking away from the cabinet, and the piece of metal that holds our fridge in place was barely hanging on.

It was nothing the prevented us from living or driving the RV, but a list of about 10 or so little things.

We sent a list of what needed to be fixed over the service department, scheduled a time to drop off our RV, and made plans to stay at my parent's house while the service shop fixed everything.

We gave them our rig for two weeks. I was able to help throw my sister's baby shower and Heath went off hunting with his dad. But after two weeks away from home, we couldn't wait to get back in the rig.

The day we were scheduled to pick up the rig, we called them to see if they were able to fix everything and set a time for pick up.

They told us they hadn't even looked at it yet.

What?! They had it for two weeks! Plus, we gave them the list of repairs before we even dropped off our home. Not to mention the fact that they knew exactly when we were picking it up.

I fully planned to give them an ear full when we picked up the RV, but conveniently the manager in charge of our rig was not on site (and wasn't around any time we called him over the next six months). There was a note on our paperwork saying they diagnosed all of our issues and ordered the parts. It clearly stated they would call when the parts came in and at that time we could return the rig for actual service.

At this point, we had to reach out to Winnebago Customer Service to let them know of the delay because the end date of our warranty passed. There was no way we were going to pay out of pocket for all of these repairs just because their service shop didn't actually service our rig.

I was beginning to expect that our dealer, Crestview RV in Buda, Texas, was delaying our repairs just so they could wait until our warranty date passed. (I have no proof of this, but it's a known issue that service departments often delay or refuse warranty work.)

Winnebago Customer Service (we called the 800 number we found online) said extending our warranty would be no problem under the circumstances and gave us a statement in writing via email, should anyone challenge us on it in the future.

And then we waited for a call from the dealer. Two weeks passed and we called the Parts Department, no answer, no reply. Then Christmas passed and we called again. And again. And then suddenly it was March, no one would take our calls, and at this point, I assume they either never ordered the parts, or ordered them, forgot about us, and used them for someone else's rig.

Either way, it was clear they were never going to fix our rig.

Fortunately, we're good friends with the folks over at Winnebago. We write blogs for Winnebago Life and they sponsor our annual RV Entrepreneur Summit each winter.

Tired of the run-around from our dealer and knowing that other service departments would likely do the same, we called up our friend Russ, a product manager at Winnebago.

We emailed him the same list we gave Crestview back in October, plus a few other things that had since started giving us issues on the rig, like our jacks.

He called back a few hours later and told us to show up at 7 AM on Monday and they could get everything fixed. **Dream. Come. True.**

Because most of our repairs fell under our warranty and because the service team over at Winnebago are real-life heroes, they did not charge us for any of our repairs.

This did mean we had to cancel our plans to spend March and April driving along the Gulf Coast of Florida and instead drive 15 Google-Maps-hours north to Forest City, back into the throws of winter. It was 100% worth it.

We had STELLAR customer service at Winnebago HQ and they have hookups in the parking lot of the service shop for overnighting. They keep a tight schedule, picking up your rig promptly at 7 AM and returning it at 3 PM.

In the future, we will only take our rig to Winnebago for service because RV service shops are notorious for...how do I say this politely...SUCKING.

Finding a Good RV Service Shop

Before I dive into more on finding the right service shop, I do want to say that Heath and I are fortunate to have very few issues with our RVs. Our first RV only broke down once and almost all of the repairs on our Winnebago fell under warranty. And while I hope you have the same luck, I want you to be fully prepared for what life on the road can look like!

Getting Serviced at Your Dealer

When searching for a service shop, the dealer where you purchased the RV is where you will likely have the most luck. All RV service shops have waitlists, many of which are months long. While traveling, we needed a few light bulbs replaced and called a local dealer in Nashville. We were told they couldn't fit us in until October. It was February!

Making an appointment with the dealer where you purchased the RV will help you skirt this waitlist. However, I know very well that sometimes they STILL won't get your repairs done. Not that I'm still bitter about it.

Service Networks and Memberships

When we purchased our Winnebago, we bought a Priority RV Network membership. This program gives you access to nationwide dealers when you are traveling.

The idea is that you can skip wait times by being a priority customer. This membership in particular is for emergency repairs. With our Winnebago, we've never needed emergency repairs (yay!).

We've also used Good Sam's Roadside Assistance program while traveling. If you're trying to decide what type of service to buy to protect yourself, I highly recommend choosing a roadside assistance program like AAA or Good Sam. We've never used our Priority Network and though it provided peace of mind while traveling, it wasn't worth the cost for us.

Avoid Chains at ALL Costs

This summer, we took our RV to Campers Inn, a chain of dealers on the east coast, for an oil change while we flew home for a funeral. All we needed was an oil change and they said they would keep our RV for a week while we were out of town.

Long story very short, they ended up charging us $400—after quoting us $150—for an oil change. This was highway robbery in itself.

But when we got to our RV after a day of flights, a horrible screeching alarm was going off. Apparently while storing our RV for a week, they left all of the batteries on. (You may remember from chapter six that you should never let your batteries die!)

Our batteries had been dead for *days* which caused all of our emergency systems in the RV to go off. There is nothing better than getting into your RV at 11 PM and hearing the piercing shriek of your propane alarm with a nice flashing "FAULT DEAD BATTERY" emergency message.

Campers Inn killed all of our batteries and we had the worst night's sleep of all time. All of this could've been avoided if the mechanics had turned off our batteries, like every other competent mechanic we've ever used.

Naturally, Camper's Inn refused to admit that killing our batteries was their fault and still charged us more than twice the quoted price.

This was not the only time we've experienced this kind of service at an RV dealership. When in doubt, scour online reviews before taking your RV to any place for service.

Also, the lack of quality service at RV shops is one of the main reasons why it's important to vet your manufacturer before choosing an RV. Our experience is that we can't rely on many RV dealerships or service shops for quality service, so we go straight to the source—Winnebago. If the dealership where you bought your RV and your manufacturer won't provide the service you need, it can be an incredibly frustrating process.

When Possible, Find a Car Mechanic

If your issue involves the chassis of your RV, car mechanics are your best chance for getting good service. We prefer car mechanics because they are more trustworthy and skilled than RV mechanics. Shocking, I know!

Plus, they are almost always cheaper! We replaced our house batteries after Campers Inn killed them for $400 at Napa Auto Parts, when every RV service shop quoted us $600.

This has been our experience time and time again and is a huge reason why we prefer rigs with engines that can be serviced at most mechanic shops. (Ford and Dodge engines are commonly used in RVs.)

Diesel Engines

If you have a diesel RV or a diesel truck, maintenance work on the road may be easier for you. Your best options for service will be truck repair shops, where the mechanics are well versed in diesel engines. These are fairly common and easy to find, especially if you are near an interstate.

Mercedes diesel engines are becoming incredibly popular with RV manufacturers lately, but owners have shared with us that service is much more difficult with these diesel rigs because you often have to go directly to a Mercedes dealership. You will, however, look slightly cooler driving a Mercedes house on wheels.

20

THE DIFFERENCE BETWEEN TRAILER PARKS, RV PARKS, AND CAMPGROUNDS

"There's a difference between RV parks and trailer parks."

I hate how often I have to explain this to friends and family. When you tell someone for the first time that you live in an RV, you see this flicker of recognition flash across a person's face as if the words "trailer trash" just bounced into their head.

There is a HUGE difference between RV parks and trailer parks, and then there are campgrounds, which can encompass a wide range of amenities. So let's break down what each of these parks look like and what makes them different.

Trailer Parks

Trailer parks are for people who live in their RV (or mobile home) full-time. There is an important distinction here between people who live in RVs full-time and full-time RVers. Full-time RVers travel. People who live in RVs full-time stay in one place, often for years.

Trailer parks are filled with trailers and fifth wheels (and *very* rarely motorhomes), but also tend to include mobile homes and more permanent structures, since residents are long term.

This means they most likely don't accept overnight campers.

There is a stigma that comes with trailer parks and unfortunately, this is what many people think about when they picture full-time RVing. In fact, a friend told us that our lifestyle opened her mind to the idea of buying an RV to travel.

"But I wouldn't want to be camping in those gross trailer parks," she said as her number one deterrent for RV life.

Odds are, if you're a full-timer, you won't be staying in trailer parks. Sure, not every RV park is the nicest place I've ever slept, but most of them are safe, clean, and sometimes extremely awesome.

RV Parks

Much like hotels, RV parks have one major target audience: vacationers. This is why it's so incredibly frustrating to find an RV park in the summer. Every nuclear American family is out traveling the countryside in a Cruise America rental RV.

Since there's something like 10,000 privately owned RV parks in the country, to make things simple I've broken down RV parks into three categories: off-the-interstate, standard, and resort.

Off-the-interstate and Long-term RV parks

These are going to be your cheapest and least desirable parks.

These parks typically are more focused on being in a convenient location and giving you a decent rate than being a fun place to hang out for a weekend. For that reason, most RV parks you see right off the highway fall into this category. These are most likely your Good Sam and Passport America parks too.

We've stayed at a lot of convenient off-the-interstate style parks and we rarely have a good experience. These are great for cheap stays when you're passing through an area, but definitely aren't places where you want to spend any length of time, even if they do only cost $15/night.

RV parks designed for long-term guests often give us the same vibes. Long-term campers tend to store a lot of, well, junk outside their RV. We ended up at one these parks recently and our neighbors had a refrigerator, a plastic slide, a broken chair, and a whole heap of other untouched items sitting outside in between our sites. It definitely kills the "let's hang out by the campfire" vibes when you're looking at someone else's garbage. But it was close to the interstate and an easy place to stop for the night.

It's worth noting that there are great RV parks for long-term guests, however, you aren't going to find them right off the interstate. Most standard RV parks offer long-term camping options, but those parks will have higher standards for what your site can look like.

These RV parks are good for inexpensive camping or you're just passing through an area, but we try to avoid these parks.

Standard RV Parks

Your standard RV park is going to be great for stays that last a weekend up to a month. These parks are going to be a little more expensive and will have a few more amenities on site.

At a standard RV park, you can count on a nightly rate from $30-$50 and basic amenities like full hookup sites, internet access, and showers. But as a step higher than your cheap, off-the-interstate parks, they will typically offer at least one amenity to make their park more attractive.

Once in Virginia, Heath and I stayed at an RV park that offered free breakfast. A park in Wisconsin had a man-made lake filled with water slides, floating trampolines, and enough pool toys to occupy kids (or two fully grown adults like ourselves) for hours. Sometimes these parks are waterfront, on rivers, lakes, and ponds.

You can count on these parks to be clean, well-kept, and generally focused on attracting vacationers, families, and retirees.

This is the most common type of campground, so odds

are as you're searching for campgrounds on the road, most will fall under this category.

RV Resorts

I'm officially spoiled. This year, Heath and I partnered with Jellystone Parks, Encore Resorts, and KOA. These parks are in the $60-$200/night range.

Why?

These are your oceanfront, restaurant and bar on-site, fishing pier, boat rental, you-literally-NEVER-need-to-leave parks.

At Sunshine Key RV Resort in the Florida Keys, we enjoyed a sunrise breakfast on a private beach. At the KOA in Myrtle Beach, we danced at live concerts on Saturday nights and took daily shuttles to the beach four blocks away. At the Jellystone Park in central Texas, they offered wine tastings and daily activities for kids.

Most of these parks are designed for vacationers and weekend warriors, but here's the rub: their off-season or long-term rates are really affordable.

In Texas Wine Country, we stay at the Jellystone Park for the winter because it has great amenities (i.e. an awesome hot tub and a small gym). It's affordable because it's their off-season. We stayed beachfront in the Keys in May, but in the winter those sites are well over $100 per night.

This is a great way to treat yourself to a luxury RV park and not pay luxury prices.

Note: All of these parks have given us free or discounted stays as part of payment for video content we produced for them. But I only say nice things about the parks that we really love!

Campgrounds

County park, state park, national park—these are typically where you find your campgrounds. Campgrounds encompass a wide range of possible amenities but they all agree on one thing: the whole point is to be in nature.

Whereas you will find RV parks in cities, off highways, and in more populated areas, campgrounds are usually reserved for the great outdoors. RV parks will often name themselves as campgrounds if they offer cabins and tent sites in addition to RV camping. (But make no mistake, these places are really just your standard RV parks.)

Campgrounds—namely state and national park campgrounds—may or may not offer hookups. I would say that you have a 50/50 shot of having electrical and water hookups and very low chances of having sewage hookups. You will also not have amenities like wifi or pools, and there may not be showers available.

But if you're at a campground, you probably don't want those things. Well, you may want a shower.

The point of campgrounds is to to be close to wildlife, hiking, kayaking, and adventure. When we visit national parks, we always try to camp in park campgrounds for this reason.

Choosing your Campsite

I'll get more into how to find RV parks and campgrounds in the next chapter. But what's important to think about is what type of camping you want to do on the road. If you're on a tight budget and plan on staying in one place, you might stay in a trailer park. If you're outdoorsy and want to explore national and state parks, then look for campgrounds. And if you're like me and you want A/C and the ability to shower daily, find a good RV park.

21

HOW TO FIND
THE RIGHT
CAMPGROUND
(AND MY
FAVORITES!)

Like I said in the last chapter, Heath and I have a bit of experience in finding both great campgrounds and really crappy ones. (You don't want to hear about the RV park where brown water came out of our faucets, trust me!)

It took us at least a year to find a good process for finding campgrounds and learning what to look for when searching for campgrounds.

How to find RV Parks

We usually type "RV parks/campgrounds near me" into Google maps to find RV parks. This will pull state and city campgrounds along with RV parks and trailer or mobile home parks. That's why it is important to know the difference between RV parks and trailer parks! Google has not yet learned the distinction.

Most higher-end RV parks are owned by corporations or franchised. The best place to find these parks will be on the corporate websites, like KOA.com, rvonthego.com (Encore Resorts), and CampJellystone.com. Passport America recently released an updated app available free in the App Store too.

Once we have a map few of parks in the area, we reference the parks' websites to check out photos and details like rates and amenities. Then it's time to check the reviews on Google, Facebook, and RV Park Reviews to see if the park is worth visiting.

If you're looking for free camping or boondocking, I'll get into the details of finding those camping options in the next chapter.

What to look for before booking

In addition to cost, there are a few things to look at when it comes to picking the right RV park, whether you're staying for a night or a few months. You can find this type of information on the park website and in reviews.

Free wifi

This is a matter of principle for me. We mostly use our own internet, but if you don't have a hotspot, be sure to make sure the park you're visiting has free wifi. You can also ask for spots close to the router if necessary.

Ability to accommodate large RVs

Even if your rig is only 35 feet, look for mention of the maximum length allowed in the park. Even in our old 29-foot rig, we drove down narrow, winding roads to RV parks that seemed too dangerous for our rig.

Beauty & Space

There are so many beautiful RV parks right on the water or tucked in a forest. There also plenty of RV parks that are nothing but a parking lot where you can see straight into your neighbor's windows. I don't have to tell you which one is better.

Trains

80% of RV parks are near train tracks. I made this stat up. But a shocking number of parks are feet away from railroad tracks which can make sleep a nightmare. Ask before booking.

Check-in & Check-out

Most RV parks have standard check-in and check-out times like hotels do. Three o'clock check-in and noon check-out are fairly standard. However, those hours are observed very loosely.

Since check out simply means driving away, you don't have to worry too much about someone knocking on your door and kicking you out if you leave at 12:15.

However, some campgrounds will charge a fee for early check-ins, especially if you're arriving before noon.

Level sites

You can't tell if the sites will be level until you arrive, but it's worth requesting a level site over the phone. These can be hard to come by!

Last month, we had a six-inch difference between the left and right side of our RV. It took all our leveling blocks, plus borrowing 2x8s from the campground to level our rig. It was incredibly frustrating to set up the rig because of this...BUT we were lakefront and there was a bald eagle that hung out by our rig every day. It's all give and take.

The little things

Great service, inexpensive washers with powerful dryers, clean restrooms with locking doors (not just shower curtains), hot tubs or indoor pools, and gift shops are all wonderful amenities at any RV park.

Reserving Your Site

When you call an RV park to reserve a site...because yes, you'll have to call since most RV parks do not offer online booking unless they are a chain or corporation like KOA...if they answer the phone, they will ask you two questions right off the bat:

> 1. How big is your rig?
> 2. 30 or 50 AMP?

Then they follow up with asking how many slides you

have, if you have pets or kids, and if you want full hook-ups (electric, water, & sewer) or partial hook-ups (electric and water only). Often times you can save a few dollars by using partial hookups and stopping by the park dump station[1] when you leave.

We rarely make advance reservations while camping, because we like the freedom to change our plans. If you prefer spontaneity like us, you should consider making advance reservations for holidays and weekends during the summer when parks will book out. We've parked in a few Walmart parking lots because we failed to make advance reservations!

How long should you stay in one place?

When you've never been somewhere before, it's often hard to estimate how long you'll want to stay in a particular area or at a particular park. Some of this will depend on services and the allowed length of stay.

At an RV park, you can stay for months at a time. This is great if you're trying to save money, considering moving to that area, or if you're looking to escape weather (i.e. snowbirding).

If you're dry camping or boondocking, you'll eventually run out of water or need to dump your tanks. We never boondock for more than 4-5 nights consecutively, but have friends who have boondocked for up to 3 weeks before refueling. Many national and state parks, including national forest or public land for boondocking, will have a two-week limit.

---

1. Most RV parks have dump stations, where you can relieve your black and grey tanks. If you spend most of your time dry camping or boondocking, RV parks will let you use their dump station for a small fee (typically under $5).

When we make our travel plans, we typically stay in an area for a week before moving on. This is about average for full-timer travel. In the past, we've traveled much more quickly, staying no more than three or four nights at a park, but this becomes exhausting. If you're working full-time or even part-time in your RV, I'd recommend staying places a minimum of a week at a time so you can easily balance work and play.

In the winter, however, all this changes.

Most RVers winter in Florida or the Southwest. Because these areas are so populated in the winter, it can be difficult to find short-term camping. Most people we know opt to stay in parks for a month or two at a time. We've rarely stayed in one place longer than two months.

Your pace of travel is totally up to your preference. The slower you travel, the less money you will likely spend. RV parks will be cheaper and you'll spend less on gas. Fast travel will allow you to see more, but will be pricier.

My Top Three RV Parks of All Time

Writing this list was nearly impossible. There are so many amazing parks out there. But if I had to choose a top three, these are it!

1. Sunshine Key Resort & Marina, Florida Keys

Beachfront campsite? Check.
Pool? Check.
Restaurant? Check.
Wifi? Check.
Ridiculously beautiful area of America with a ton of things to do in the area? Check.
This campground is currently closed after Hurricane

Irma, but should re-open in 2018. Hands down, this was the most beautiful campground we've ever visited.

There's another nearby RV resort on Fiesta Key that is run by the same company, but I didn't want my whole top three list to all be in the Florida Keys! Fiesta Key did, however, have an awesome tiki bar on the beach with killer piña coladas, so I'm kind of confused as to why I don't live there full-time.

2. Normandy Farms Campground, Foxborough, Massachusetts

This campground is insane. We've stayed here twice in our travels and each time I visit, it blows me away.

Four pools, three hot tubs, sauna, gym, tennis courts, 18-hole frisbee golf course, softball field, and the crowning glory: their spa.

During our most recent stay, I pampered myself with a 60-minute massage and it. was. glorious. This was my first time visiting an RV park so luxurious it offered an entire spa and it didn't disappoint.

And to make it all that much sweeter, this giant park is only $50/night, a steal for the amenities. Plus, even though the park itself is huge, there are lots of trees, fields, and ponds to make it not feel like a giant parking lot.

3. Myrtle Beach Travel Park, North Myrtle Beach, South Carolina

This is the ideal summer vacation RV park. There were multiple pools, a lazy river, two restaurants on site, and our site had a view of the lake from our front window and the ocean from our back window.

But most importantly, this park was north of the crazy, packed beaches that Myrtle Beach is known for and incredibly private and quiet. We visited in May and the weather was perfect. With miles of beach stretching in each direction, I instantly fell in love with this park.

Honorable mention:

- Texas Wine Country Jellystone Park, Fredericksburg, Texas
- Miami Everglades Resort, Miami, Florida
- Narrows Too, Bar Harbor, Maine
- Nugget RV Park in St. Regis, Montana

How to Find Campgrounds

Finding campgrounds follows much of the above process, although campgrounds are typically easier to find. National park websites will have web pages listing all the available campgrounds in the park, along with pertinent information like length limits and hookup options. Many state parks will only offer one or two campgrounds within the park, which makes finding campsites easy.

Many RVers worry that they will be unable to visit parks due to the size of their RV. For the most part, you will not have to worry about this. We've visited 16/59 national parks in America (plus many state and national parks in western Canada) and we've always been able to take our 33-feet rig through the park. While size may restrict which campground you can visit, most parks can accommodate you at one or more campgrounds.

If you have a larger rig and are nervous about visiting a park, I highly recommend calling a ranger before you visit. They can answer your questions and give you directions to help you avoid any limited access roads.

Reserving Your Site

Most state and national park campgrounds operate on a first-come, first-served basis. Some parts of some campgrounds are reservable online, but the reservation process is clunky and confusing. We opt for first-come, first served, and we can usually find a campsite if it isn't a weekend. However, this is stressful. If you're planning a road trip and want to guarantee a stay at a certain park, book ahead.

Our Favorite Campgrounds

1. Tunnel Mountain Village 1 Campground, Banff National Park, Alberta, Canada

Banff is the most beautiful place I've ever visited and this campground offers incredible mountain views. Plus a bear casually strolled by while we sipped on our coffee one morning. Nature is wild.

2. Kirk Creek Campground, Los Padres National Forest, Big Sur, California

Campgrounds along the Pacific Coast Highway book out six months in advance. We didn't know that when we started our scenic drive three years ago. We passed dozens of campgrounds, all of which were full.

But we lucked out when a ranger took pity on us. Someone had paid for a three-night reservation but had never shown up. So the ranger gave us the last night (though he still made us pay). This campground is on the cliffs of Big Sur, and you can listen to the waves hitting the rocks while you fall asleep.

3. Signal Mountain Campground, Grand Teton National Park, Wyoming

This campground has crazy lake and mountain views—if your RV is under 30 feet. We camped here in our first rig, which was 29-feet in length. Two deer came up to our window while I was cooking soup (in July, because it gets COLD in the Tetons) and Heath jumped in the lake as his "shower" since we didn't have hookups. He said it was the coldest water he's ever been in, but with the best view.

22

HOW TO FIND
FREE CAMPING

RV parks might not be your thing. I know that after a summer of visiting RV parks, I'm begging for open land and boondocking.

Before we dig into finding free camping, let's go over some quick RV camping terms you'll hear often:

Dry camping: This is where you camp with "no hookups" meaning you don't have shore power, water, or sewer. Typically one refers to dry camping when camping at state or national parks. You likely still have to pay fees for dry camping.

Boondocking: The definition of boondocking is different depending on who you talk to. There are a few aspects to it:

1. You must be dry camping.

2. It's free. You can boondock in Walmart parking lots, rest areas, or in friend's driveways.
3. (Debatable) You're far from other people or RVers, typically in the wilderness or on free public lands.

Moochdocking: This is where you camp on driveways or private land—usually owned by a friend, relative, or I don't know, maybe you like staying with strangers—for free. You may or may not have electricity or water.

For many people, boondocking and dry camping is preferred because you can save money and be more in touch with nature. RV parks can sometimes be crowded or loud, so we find ourselves dry camping or boondocking when we need a break from the masses.

If you remember from part two, this is when you'll want to make sure you have a generator or solar power as a power source for your rig.

How to Find Boondocking

Campendium

This is my #1 resource for finding free camping and boondocking. They have a huge database of different types of camping, plus reviews, pricing details, and photos. They make it easy to research free campsites and you can filter on their website for "free camping".

However, the best thing about Campendium are the detailed reviews. They note cell signal strength, post camper photos, note the latest pricing, and tips for navigating to off-the-beaten-path sites. When looking for camping on BLM or National Forest land, this is always our first stop.

AllStays

This app is the cream of the crop. It costs $10, but pays for itself in one night of free camping. It keeps one of the most up to date campground directories available. We typically use it to find Walmart, Kmart, Lowes, and other parking lots that allow overnight camping. The reviews in the app are great for finding the right overnight stop.

US Public Lands App

This app was built by RV bloggers Technomadia and helps you find BLM (Bureau of Land Management) and USFS (US Forest Service) land where you can boondock for free. The app costs $2.99 (at the moment that I am typing this) and can give you great details on public lands and how to know if you're accidentally trespassing somewhere.

Boondockers Welcome

If you want to moochdock with strangers, look no further than Boondockers Welcome. This annual membership is a great way to find driveway camping. Many of the people who list property on Boondockers are RVers themselves and generally awesome people.

Call the experts

Find a local BLM regional office and give them a call. Park rangers have so much information they'll be able to give you on different places you can and cannot camp.

Check Instagram

The real experts. There is no better place to find gorgeous boondocking locations than Instagram right now. My feed is always filled with shots of RVs on dirt roads tucked away in the mountains. If you want to find great boondocking sites, ask the people who do this every day! Many travelers are great at replying to comments on Instagram or will location-tag their camping location so you can add it to your list of future destinations.

Boondocking Etiquette

Whether you're in a parking lot or in the forest, there are a few rules that you should follow before you pop out your slides and build a campfire.

Make sure you're in the right place.

Sites like Campendium will offer exact coordinates so that you park in the right area. The goal with boondocking is to experience nature, not destroy it. Make sure that you use existing roads and stay in designated camping areas.

Drive your tow car into new camping spots to scout first.

If you're worried about your rig being able to get down a dirt road, you can always disconnect your tow car and scout a location first. This is a great way to not end up in a tight spot. This is also where using Campendium reviews or asking fellow travelers will come in handy!

Leave no trace.

Primitive and wild camping means you won't have a ranger or camp host around to make sure you're cleaning up your stuff. Don't abuse nature. Pick up your things when you leave.

This also means that you should never dump your black tanks when boondocking. Never, never, NEVER. In addition to being disgusting and bad for the environment, it also ruins the camping experience for everyone else. Don't be a bad seed!

Don't overstay your welcome and be respectful of surroundings.

Anywhere you park will have limits. For most public land, the limit is 14 nights within a 28 day period. There will be signs or information on stay limits on any of the previously mentioned apps and websites.

Not overstaying your welcome and being respectful also applies to overnight parking in places like Walmart or Cabela's. Most of these businesses are kindly allowing you to park for free for one night. Don't open up all your slides, put your jacks down, slide out your awning, and throw a party outside. It's also customary to shop at the store and ask the manager if you can camp before you settle in for the night.

Check local laws and rules.

Be sure to check for burn bans, wildlife warnings, vehicle limitations, and other restrictions before boondocking.

Be respectful of your neighbors.

When boondocking in the Tetons, we made sure to park

at the far left end of an open, flat field. This not only allowed plenty of room for other RVs to enjoy the space, but it also ensured that we wouldn't have someone parking right next to us. Especially when you are in wide open spaces, give your neighbors plenty of room.

And while this may be common sense, you should avoid playing loud music or running your generator at all hours of the night. Some camping areas will have rules against generators or loud music even. But in general, it's best to preserve the peace of an area by avoiding these two loud activities.

Be conservative.

When you're camping off the grid, supplies are limited. Conserve water. Don't use a ton of power (unless you're equipped with solar). And avoid filling your grey and black tanks.

We have never showered while boondocking for this reason. We will use baby wipes or Epic Wipes, which are 16 times the size of a baby wipe and great for a full body "shower" when you are conserving water.

Be prepared.

Before boondocking, you should always empty your grey and black tanks and fill your fresh water tank. Buy groceries and any other supplies you may need for camping off the grid. Oh, and do your laundry! There's nothing worse than camping in the mountains, running out of underwear, and not being able to shower.

23

BUILDING COMMUNITY ON THE ROAD

Three years ago we were in St Louis, Missouri and the fridge in our old RV had just blown up. We were stressed, to say the least.

One of our favorite authors and fellow full-time traveler, Chris Guillebeau, was hosting a book tour five hours away in Nashville. It wasn't exactly on our route to Chicago, but we decided to go anyway. We knew that an evening with friends and meeting new people would be good for us.

While on the way, we tweeted a picture to Chris and told him we were driving our RV to his book signing. He was excited and shared it with several of his friends who were going to be there. Once we arrived, we instantly made friends, had people buy us drinks, and after the signing, we hosted an impromptu tour of our RV.

Today, several people we met at that book signing are some of our closest friends to this day. We've even convinced a few of those friends to try RVing!

We've realized that community on the road is all about expanding our comfort zone and redefining what friendship looks like. We drove five hours out of our way to meet up with Chris because we knew that he attracts awesome people that would love and understand RV life.

While we have lost many old friendships since we started traveling, we've made new friends who share similar values with us. Friends who share our love of travel, entrepreneurship, and living a life of adventure.

The key is intentionality. Most of the time, community on the road means we have to go out of our way to hang out with old friends or to meet new ones. We've actually met up with our friends Kristin and Jason Snow on the side of the road *twice* as we drove in opposite directions. That's what making friends looks like sometimes!

Making friends and building community on the road isn't easy, but there are a few great ways to meet and make friends while traveling.

Invite friends and family to meet you on the road!

This is the easiest way to combat loneliness or homesickness on the road. Bring home to you!

At our first ever RV park, our new neighbors imparted some valuable knowledge to us about RV occupancy. Regardless of how many your RV can physically sleep, the rule of thumb is this: you can host 6 people for drinks, 4 people for dinner, and only 2 people for sleep. To put it simply, they recommended never hosting people overnight in the RV. It's just too small!

Well a couple months after buying our Winnebago, we decided to give hosting a try. My husband's best friend flew into Nashville (we, of course, drove the RV to the airport to pick him up) and we spent the weekend camping in Great Smoky National Park.

We were a mixture of nervous and excited to host in the RV for the first time. Hosting friends or family can be tricky—especially when you have to teach them basics like how to flush the toilet—but we absolutely loved it! We've slept up to five people in the RV and while it's a little cramped, the community is worth it. It's the best way to share our love of RV life with our favorite people.

There's only one catch: when friends and family meet you on the road, it is typically their vacation. Since we work on the road, this makes it especially hard for us to get any work done while we have visitors!

Facebook groups

Our biggest source of community is our Facebook group: Make Money and RV. (I know, spammiest title ever right? But Heath made it without me!)

I've met thousands of people through our group and made a lot of really amazing friends that I never otherwise could've met. A few other great Facebook groups for RVers are RV to Freedom, Internet for RVers, and Full-time Families.

Owner groups on Facebook are also great resources for information! We are in the Winnebago Brave owners group, so when we have questions about our RV, we can ask that community for advice.

RV clubs and memberships

We talked about Escapees RV Club back in chapter 18 as a source of community on the road, but there is no end to the number of RV clubs and membership communities. Escapees and their related club for younger RVers, Xscapers, both host rallies and community events across the country. Winnebago has WIT Club, a community for Winnebago owners to get together, with chapters in almost every state. And there's Fulltime Families, a membership community for anyone traveling with kids.

RV clubs can be a little more tricky to find, but if you're in any Facebook group about RVing, members will be more than happy to share their favorite RV clubs and memberships.

Follow RV bloggers

Many of our favorite friends today we met through our blog. We read and reply to almost every comment, email, and message we receive, and we've built so many friendships this way.

Following RV bloggers is the easiest way to meet new people, mostly because bloggers often hold meetups. This past winter, Heath and I wrote in our email newsletter where we were snowbirding. We had over 20 people end up camping at that RV park during our stay to hang out with us, which was unexpected, to say the least.

So we grilled out and hosted potlucks and went on hikes together and we made a lot of good friends that way. Just last night, we met up with 30 strangers and other RVers at a meetup we hosted in Nashville.

This is a great way for us to take our community offline and meet in person. We started our RV Entrepreneur

Summit, a business conference for RVers, in 2017 as another way for us to bring our community together.

Instagram

If I had a dollar for every time Heath said, *I invited over this couple I met on Instagram to have dinner with us...* But strangely enough, his strategy works.

Instagram is ultra popular with van lifers, but there's quite a few of us RVers on Instagram too. We've met quite a few of our friends and most our podcast guests on Instagram. Here's how we do it:

1. Search for popular hashtags like #rvlife #rvers or #rving or search your location.

Depending on if you're looking for people who share your lifestyle or your current zip code, this is the place to start.

2. Follow, like, and comment on cool posts.

It's important to not appear to be a spammer. Anyone can comment with an emoji or say "cool pic" or "looks fun". In fact, that's what a spambot does, if you're into paying for a program that will comment on other's posts. If you're trying to get to know real people, leave thoughtful comments like a real-life likable human being.

3. Refresh app every five seconds to see if anyone has responded to your comments.

Oh, normal people don't do this?

4. Interact enough to be considered Instagram friends and find out where they are traveling in a non-creepy way.

If you just know their Insta handle and not their names, you aren't friends yet.

5. Hang out in real life!

Once you meet in real life, badda-bing, badda-boom! Now you have new best friends.

While you can follow this same technique on Facebook, Twitter, and other social media, Instagram makes it easiest to find fellow travelers.

Caravanning

Once you befriend other travelers online, it's time to hang out! We have only caravanned once and we LOVED it. Caravanning is great because, unlike hosting, you can retire to your RV if you need time alone.

We caravanned with our friends Mark and Gaby from Grand Teton National Park all the way north to Canada. Because we work on the road, we spent half the day on our computers and the other half of the day exploring. The best part of caravanning with these cool kids was experiencing and learning new things. We drove up a tiny dirt road in the mountains to boondock on BLM land we found on Campendium. We built a fire and learned night photography tricks from Mark. And we kayaked down the Snake River together in the Tetons.

It was an amazing week and we were able to enjoy it all while still running our businesses.

Get outside!

Travelers are the friendliest people! All it takes to make friends in a campground is to be that couple roasting s'mores outside or walking around the campground with a glass of wine. Most RVers are friendly and eager to connect with other campers on the road. So walk out of your RV, explore your campground or RV park, and make new friends!

EPILOGUE

Sometimes I can't believe that I live and travel in an RV full-time. Pretty sure my parents can't believe it either.

Traveling these past three years with Heath, we've had the best time of our lives. We visited over a dozen national parks, many of which we had never heard of before. We've swam in the Pacific and the Atlantic and we even dipped our toes in the glacial lakes of northern Canada. We've camped on glaciers and summited mountains.

We've done so many things that never would've been possible without our RV and a little sense of wanderlust.

If you're thinking about RV travel, just do it. Do it now so that like us, you can make everyone scratch their heads and assume we are some weird online millionaires or hippies (I'm happily neither).

I've heard a lot of opinions on my lifestyle in the past few years, but this comment—that I hear often—is my favorite:

> **"You're so smart to do this now. I wish I had started sooner."**

Start sooner. Jump in. Take a risk. You're better off than me, the girl who has still never touched our sewer hose.

GLOSSARY

If you're new to RV life, you'll quickly start hearing RVing terms thrown around that you're fully expected to know. And you feel awkward asking what these words mean because you're pretty sure you don't WANT to know what a black tank is.

Here are the top 31 RVing terms I hear most often that need to be explained. Settle in, because RVers make up some WEIRD words!

Full-Timers or Full-Timing

The crazy people who live and travel in an RV all. the. time.

Part-timers

The slightly less crazy people who travel in their RV primarily for vacations. Also called weekend warriors.

Toad

This is not an amphibian! Your toad is the car you tow behind your motorhome. This is sometimes referred to as a dinghy. This term is pretty exclusively used in referring to towing with motorhomes and not with trailers.

Fiver or 5er

A fifth wheel.

Triple Tow

This is when you tow two things! (Kind of confusing, right?) This can look crazy and is illegal in some states. State Lines App is great for learning where this is legal.

Examples: A truck towing a fifth wheel towing a boat or a motorhome towing a trailer towing a car. We've seen both and YIKES.

Dually

A truck with four tires on the rear axle (six tires total). Most commonly seen towing a fiver.

Rig

Slang reference for RV. This could be a trailer, camper, or motorhome.

Coach

Another slang reference for RV, but typically referencing motorhomes.

Diesel Pusher

A diesel motorhome where the engine is in the back of the rig.

Toy Hauler

An RV with a space to store your badass toys like motorcycles, ATVs, or dirt bikes. Or whatever fancy toys you
like. A toy hauler can be a trailer, fiver, or motorhome.

Basement

The storage area beneath your RV. Also referred to as
bays or understorage or the place where your store all
your poop hoses.

Blackwater

The wastewater from your toilet.

Grey Tank

The wastewater from the sinks and shower drains.

Fresh Water Tanks

The fresh water you keep on board for use when you do
not have water hookups.

Holding Tanks

Holding tanks is a term used to refer to your grey, black,
and fresh water tanks.

Honeywagon

The magical and smelly mobile tank offered at RV parks
that will pump your sewer system. Most commonly

found in RV parks that don't offer sewer hookups at every site.

Shore Power

The electricity you get when you plug your RV into an outlet

FHU or Full Hookups

When you have access to water, sewer, and electric at a campsite.

Slide-outs

The sections of your motorhome that slide out when you are parked. We have opposing slides in our RV that give us so much extra space! Also referred to as slides or pop-outs.

LP

Propane (or liquified petroleum, in case you wondered what LP actually stands for).

TT

This one is tricky! Look for context clues. This could mean Thousand Trails, an RV membership, or travel trailer, a type of tow-behind RV.

Wheelbase

The distance between your axles. This is an important number to know as it greatly affects your turn radius!

Dry Camping

This is where you camp with "no hook ups" meaning you don't have shore power, water, or sewer. Typically one refers to dry camping when camping at state or national parks. You likely still have to pay fees for dry camping.

Boondocking

The definition of boondocking is different depending on who you talk to. There are a few aspects to it:

> 1. You must be dry camping.
> 2. It's free. You can boondock in Walmart parking lots, rest areas, or in friend's driveways.
> 3. (Debatable) You're far from other people or RVers, typically in the wilderness or on free public lands. See primitive camping below.

Moochdocking

This is where you camp on driveways or private land—usually owned by a friend, relative, or I don't know maybe you like staying with strangers—for free. You may or may not have electricity or water.

Boondockers Welcome is a great place to look for moochdocking, especially if you like strangers.

Primitive Camping

Primitive camping, also sometimes called wild camping, is when you boondock in the middle of nowhere! Can also be synonymous with boondocking.

Sticks-and-bricks (also referred to as S&B)

Sticks-n-bricks, or S&B if you're really hip, are buildings, typically houses, made of...wait for it...sticks and bricks. Basically any home that isn't on wheels.

Brick-and-mortar

Same as above, but used by the slightly less hip people. Just kidding! Typically brick-and-mortar is more commonly used in referring to businesses than homes.

Snowbirding

Snowbirds are the human versions of real birds. They fly (drive) south for the winter!

Workamper© or Workamping

A type of work exchange where you work for an RV park or campground in exchange for free or subsidized rent as well as pay. Can be used to refer to anyone working a seasonal job, but typically reserved for those working at RV parks.

RV Entrepreneur

Anyone who travels in an RV while running their own business.

FAQ: SHORT ANSWERS TO THE MOST POPULAR #RVLIFE QUESTIONS

In case I didn't mention it or you just need a refresher, here are 30 quick answers to the top questions people ask us.

1. What RV should I buy?

I don't care. Whatever one you like. It's your house dude.

2. What manufacturer should I buy? Which ones should I avoid?

Winnebago and Coachmen are the brands we've purchased and both are high quality and highly durable. Thor has the worst reputation (and the best prices, of course) and I would never recommend them. (My friend's cabinets literally fell from the ceiling and crashed into his floor while he was driving. They are cheap for a reason, folks.)

3. Why did you choose a motorhome?

We didn't own a truck to tow a trailer and we didn't want a truck payment. Plus since we visited all 50 states in our first year, we wanted something that was easy to get up and go. That meant a Class C rig with no slide-outs.

4. Did Winnebago give you your RV for free?

No. I wish.

5. How can I convince [insert name of RV manufacturer here] to give me a free RV?

You won't. Most companies ignore these types of requests. Heck, Winnebago turned down the Kardashians. If they aren't getting a free rig, you won't either.

6. How do you get packages?

I send them to the RV park where I'm staying or if we are boondocking, to the UPS store for pick up ($5 fee).

7. How do you receive checks or get paid?

When people pay us by check, we give them my parents' address. I wouldn't risk sending checks to an RV park unless I know we are going to be there for a while. (Why is it that it takes longer for checks to arrive than any other mail?!)

If a physical check isn't necessary, we have clients pay us via PayPal, Cash app, or Venmo.

8. How do you get internet?

Black market. Let me know if you need a hook up at info@heathandalyssa.com.

9. How do you watch the Cowboys' games?

I don't think I ever covered cable hookups in this guide, probably because it's not 2002 and we don't watch live television. Most RVs will have a coax cable hookup and an antenna. 90% of RV parks will offer basic cable, and some will offer more. You'll need to supply your own cable cord, but you'll be able to watch football all weekend long.

10. What's your MPG?

Depressing, that's what it is.

Most larger RVs average 6-10 mpg. This will be on the lower end if you have full tanks onboard and if you tow a vehicle. Diesel engines tend to get better gas mileage, as do smaller rigs.

11. Does your RV have a bathroom?

Would I live in it if it didn't?

12. A shower?

See above.

13. How do you do laundry?

I've never visited an RV park without laundry services available. Many campgrounds offer this too. I once watched a moose and her two babies walk by while I was washing clothes in Denali National Park.

14. Do you need a special license to drive a motorhome?

For most rigs, no. It has to do with weight and state law. Likely, you won't have to worry about this.

15. How do you cook meals?

Our rig has a three-burner stove and an oven big enough to fit a 13×9 pan. I can cook anything in our rig, including roasting a whole chicken, steaming vegetables, popping homemade popcorn, and making lots and lots of tacos. So far the only thing I haven't mastered is chocolate chip cookies. I did make a killer funfetti cake for our anniversary, so it's time I give cookies another try. The key is to line the bottom of your pan with foil so the flame of the propane oven doesn't crisp the bottom of your food!

16. Do you ever feel unsafe?

Nah. RV parks are different than trailer parks. RV parks are typically destinations for retirees or families. The most unsafe I have ever felt was when we camped in Yellowstone with all our windows open and I was pretty sure a bear was going to smell me and break down the door to eat me. Never happened though.

17. Where do you park the RV when you fly?

I wrote a whole post on this, because there are a lot of options and I know the secret to free RV storage. You can read it on our website: https://heathandalyssa.com/three-places-leave-the-rv-when-flying/

18. Do you really stay in Walmart parking lots?

Yep, typically when we are breaking up drive days and can't find an RV park. You can level the jacks, pop out the slides, invite 20 friends over for a BBQ, and Walmart could care less. The law on this, however, is county based. There will be posted signs if you cannot stay overnight. All Stays is a great ($10) app that will let you know about Walmarts, Cabela's, Sam's, Kmarts, Lowes, etc. that allow overnight parking in your area.

19. What do you do to make money on the road?

I run HeathandAlyssa.com where we have a blog, podcast, and YouTube channel—plus books like this one. I also run Padgett Creative LLC, our video production company. Heath does freelance marketing consulting and is the CEO and co-founder of CampgroundBooking.com, his software startup.

20. Can you take [insert job here] on the road?

Probably, yes. Unless you're a nanny. That would be kidnapping.

For more on working on the road and how to do it, check out Heath's podcast, The RV Entrepreneur, where he interviews entrepreneurs who travel full-time in their RV.

21. Do you ever get tired of living in a small space?

I miss a bathtub and dishwasher, but the small space has never bothered me.

22. How often do you boondock versus staying in RV parks?

Totally depends on the part of the country. Boondocking is easier in the west and the south where there are more wide open places. We love boondocking, but sometimes it's nice to have electricity and endless water. However, we've spent the past two months in RV parks, and we are beyond ready for some open spaces on BLM land.

23. Where can you boondock?

There are so many options! We use two main resources for finding boondocking:

All Stays app: It'll cost $10 and save you that money a million times over.

Campendium.com: This is a free website that will give you reviews and coordinates of free (and paid) sites. There are RV park listings here too, but it's the best place I've found for reliable listings for BLM (Bureau of Land Management) or National Forest land.

24. How do you stay in shape on the road?

We had a Planet Fitness membership during our first year on the road because they have the most locations nationwide and it's only $20/month to access all their gyms. Now we have our kayaks and bikes and hiking boots to keep us active!

25. Will you travel when you have kids?

I don't know the future!!!

26. How long do you stay in one place?

It totally depends. We usually move weekly during the summer and opt for 1-3 month stays in the fall and winter months.

27. What's your favorite state?

California is the most beautiful BUT the most RV-unfriendly. But they have the perfect blend of ocean, mountains, and desert. Runners-up are Alaska, Vermont, and Maine.

28. What's the best road trip in America?

1. The Florida Keys
2. The Road to Alaska
3. Pacific Coast Highway

29. How do you handle finances on the road?

Many people assume that it's hard to file your taxes when you live in an RV. I have no idea why they think this.

We file our taxes with a CPA every spring. We have done this in Texas (where we are domiciled) and we have done this on the road, mailing or emailing in relevant documents to our accountant.

We also bank with Chase for both our personal and business accounts, so we can have nationwide banking access.

30. What are the best days to travel? And the best time to arrive at campgrounds?

These are tricky little questions! When choosing your travel days, beware of holidays, cities on your route, and rush hour. Way too often have we forgotten to think about what cities we might drive through on our route and ended up hitting 4:00 PM traffic on the interstate.

Generally, Saturdays and weekdays are the best days for travel. Fridays and Sundays are generally the worst and never, ever try to drive your RV during rush hour in a city! It's too much stress.

When planning your arrival at a campground, keep the above rules in mind. Most campgrounds allow you to start checking in to your site between 1:00 PM and 3:00 PM and you should always aim to check in before sunset and/or before the office closes. Parking your RV in the dark at an RV park you've never visited before, well, sucks.

Checking in earlier is also key at state or national parks which typically operate on a first-come, first-served basis. The earlier you arrive, the better site you can find!

RESOURCES

Before you buy your first RV...

We highly recommend renting an RV before you fully commit to the lifestyle. We recommend two peer-to-peer rental companies (and we do NOT recommend Cruise America under any circumstances).

- Outdoorsy: We've rented our own RV out on Outdoorsy and have loved working with this company!
- RV Share

Towing Necessities

- A Blue Ox Alpha Tow Bar
- A Blue OX Base Plate
- A Blue OX light kit
- Brake Buddy auxiliary braking system

RV Essentials

These are all things you will actually 100% need and use for your RV, based on our experiences.

- Sewer Hose
- Electrical adapter

- 30 AMP extension cord
- Leveling blocks
- Toilet deodorant (NEVER travel without this!)
- Drinking water hose
- Water filter
- Water pressure regulator
- Hose connector
- Collapsable ladder—not all RVs come with a ladder attached!

RV Memberships

- Good Sam
- Passport America
- Escapees
- Thousand Trails
- Harvest Hosts

Community

- Escapees Club
- Our Facebook Group: The RV Entrepreneur
- Full-time Families
- RV to Freedom Facebook Group

Internet on the Road

- weBoost Cell Booster: This will jump your signal from one bar to three, like pure magic. (We use the 4G-X model specifically for RVs!)
- Internet for RVers Facebook Group
- RV Mobile Internet

Go-to Apps for the Road

- **Co-Pilot GPS:** Offline GPS specific for RVs to make sure you avoid low clearances
- **Passport America:** Great for finding PA parks
- **Snapseed:** For photo editing on the go
- **Spotify:** Never struggle with radio dials again!
- **Coverage:** Maps for finding cell coverage
- **State Lines:** You know what's annoying? Not knowing different state laws and not being allowed to buy wine before noon. This app will let you know all the basic laws in every state.
- **Gas Buddy:** Everyone's go-to for cheap gas
- **Overcast:** Keep your drive days more exciting by listening to podcasts, like Heath's ?
- **MyRadar:** You will NEED a good radar app for inclement weather
- **Hurdlr:** A free app that will help track business expenses on the road

More Resources from HeathandAlyssa.com

The RV Entrepreneur School: Every month we publish courses on RVing and business. You can see all courses at heathandalyssa.com/school

The RV Entrepreneur Podcast: This is Heath's weekly podcast where he interviews full-time RVers on how they make money on the road.

The RV Entrepreneur Book: If you want something more in-depth and tactical than the podcast interviews, read Heath's book where he breaks down actionable steps for building a business on the road.

Heath & Alyssa on Youtube: We just started our Youtube channel and are focusing on creating videos that inspire you to not only travel and experience more, but to capture these moments so you never forget them.

Hourly America: During our first year on the road, I filmed a documentary where Heath worked a different job in all fifty states during our travels. We made it free for you to watch on Facebook!

ACKNOWLEDGEMENTS

This guide would still be on the desktop of my computer if it weren't for constant encouragement from my beloved Heath Padgett. You're the best partner, cheerleader, and husband. Thanks for putting up with me through the stress of launching this book and loving me always.

Thank you to all of our readers, listeners, and fellow full-timers who asked me the same questions so many times that I had to write a book to fit in all my answers. Shout out to The RV Entrepreneur Facebook group for being so wonderfully supportive and engaged. I write for you guys.

HUGE thank you to Teresa Ott for giving me invaluable information how to actually format this thing. Thanks to Greg Self for fixing all my typos and making me sound smarter. And all the applause emojis to Kelsey Henry for actually laughing out loud while proofreading my book and making me feel like a million dollars. Thank you so much to Suzann Lankford for creating the beautiful artwork on my book cover!

Thank you to Donald Miller, Jeff Goins, and Ally Fallon for writing the books that inspired my wanderlust and got me thinking that I needed a little more adventure in my life.

And finally, thank you to all the s'mores I ate while writing this book. You da real MVP.

ABOUT THE AUTHOR

In 2014, Alyssa con-
vinced her husband
Heath to take her to all
50 states for our honey-
moon and somehow he
tricked her into doing it
all in an RV. They've
lived and traveled in an
RV ever since.

Alyssa is a travel
blogger, film producer,
and the chief navigator
and co-pilot of their
Winnebago.

She directed and
produced *Hourly America* a documentary film about their
50 state honeymoon that was featured on CBS, CNN,
Fox, People, Yahoo, Huffington Post, and more.

A Beginner's Guide to Living in an RV, an Amazon best-
seller, is her first self-published book.

Alyssa is originally from Denton, Texas, but has been
RVing for so long that she never knows what to say when
someone says "where are you from?"

Made in the USA
Columbia, SC
10 August 2019